**Management Skills Series**
Health and Safety

**Other titles in the Management Skills series:**
Alfred York: *Managing for Success: A Human Approach*
Seraydarian and Pywell: *Successful Business Writing*
Gordon F. Gatiss: *Total Quality Management*

# Health and Safety

## A Guide for the Newly Appointed

JOHN R. MORRIS

CASSELL

IN ASSOCIATION WITH THE INSTITUTE FOR SUPERVISION AND MANAGEMENT

**Cassell**
Wellington House, 125 Strand, London WC2R 0BB
370 Lexington Avenue, New York, NY 10017-6550

© John R. Morris, 1997

First published 1997
Reprinted 1998

**British Library Cataloguing-in-Publication Data**
A catalogue record for this book is available from the British Library.

ISBN 0-304-70120-3 (paperback)

Typeset by Kenneth Burnley at Irby, Wirral, Cheshire.
Printed and bound in Great Britain by Redwood Books, Trowbridge, Wiltshire

310112

# Contents

# Foreword

## Safety Training – a Legal Responsibility for All

Safety as a central agent of management discipline has been a long time jostling for a place on the top table. The 1974 Health and Safety at Work Act, which remains our main controlling law, involved a laundry list of management responsibilities. The employer's duty of care had to be exercised through a safe workplace; plant; use, handling and storage of materials; place of work, including access and movement; working environment; the provision of information, training and supervision for employees; and, finally, safe systems of work, unspecified, in the plural. Nowhere in the legislation was the point made, that without co-ordination from the top, the whole management structure of the plant would be vulnerable.

The depth of this vulnerability was dramatically revealed in a succession of disasters hitting British industry in the late 1980s. One official enquiry after another trenchantly criticized the directors of major companies. In some cases there appeared to be no one person with overall responsibility for controlling safety. Cumulatively defective departmental safety systems went unnoticed at the top until catastrophe struck. Hundreds of lives were lost as an oil platform roof blew off, trains crashed into each other, and a ferry ship turned over. These embarrassing events played their part in shaping public opinion in support of the tighter legislation which is now in force.

The new European-integrated legislation has subsequently imposed a duty on all managers, from the top downwards, and operatives to be trained in their safety responsibilities. Managers needing technical or specialist skills are required to get appropriate qualifications, but all managers and operatives on routine jobs must have the necessary training to do their jobs competently.

## Production – a Mutually Testing Experience

In setting out to brief line managers on running a safe system of work, it is important to see the problem in its full context. Productive work is a partnership between humanity and mother nature. Mother nature possesses a large and generous bosom, and nourishes us all; but she has fangs and claws to match. In the world economy in which we now have to survive, we have to face both these aspects of her. The beneficial qualities of natural forces like steam, electricity and nuclear power which drive our machines, light our streets and rooms, and keep us warm, have to be matched against the trips, falls, fires and explosions that are closely associated with them. The two mutually destructive elements are found in mother nature's favourite progeny, ourselves. As managers, or perhaps, mismanagers of the global economy, which now provides the framework for international production, we find ourselves struggling to keep in balance a developing world with many booming industries, and an undeveloped world in a state of political and economic dissolution.

Pushing the context of safety management this far out is no theoretical extravaganza. The growth of global warming from industrial and chemical emissions is now recognized by some as literally putting the planet at risk. Cutting back these emissions demands effective world economic and political co-ordination. In this fractured and, over large areas, disintegrating world structure few people would argue that managing its say can be easy. Yet achieving this is now an issue, but not only for the politicians. It is a day-to-day practical problem for the British chemical and power industries and for everyone of us using fuel-powered vehicles.

## Trouble in the Shop and Round the Corner

The disruptive impact from world friction is not just an issue of the wider ecological environment. Within our own localities, shopkeepers and garage staff are no less vulnerable to the weaknesses of the surrounding social system. Vandals, thieves, arsonists, and terrorists are all part of this troubled world. The facts have to be faced: no workplace can be completely safe, anywhere. Individual producers may feel secure on their own local patch and under their own sturdy roofs, but the world around and under them is becoming increasingly shaky.

The concept of total quality assurance – 'getting it right first time' has been internationally recognized as a vital management tool. Systematic auditing both removes the risks and ensures that standards can be steadily raised to advance along with technology. Getting at the causes of harm and not having to cope with their effects removes the need to clean up any resulting mess. But there remain areas of work and of management which are difficult to incorporate fully within this process. It can work with companies with stable markets, highly audited and controlled safety management systems and securely guarded premises. Small firms, at the rough and tumble end of the market, have none of these stabilities. Even with effective internal management, they are frequently vulnerable to external threats and pressures from customers and the public. Work situations for contractors are often unfamiliar; the types of work change from contract to contract; and the equipment is hired in and operated by sub-contractors arriving fresh on each job. Performance auditing remains an important management tool, but it is more difficult to apply and very much less reliable in its effects. None of these small firms can pretend that breakdowns or break-ins cannot occur. Procedures at the ready to deal with these situations are essential.

## Big Producers Vulnerable Too

Small working units can no longer be seen as a diminishing element in the productive system. The self-employed contractor and the short-term appointments are now rapidly replacing the traditional job-for-life employees. The community structure of work is unravelling before our eyes. But the big producers are also vulnerable, even with highly organized safety systems. Emergency services have a no less active role in a large proportion of companies using chemicals with hazardous wastes which could cause environmental and ecological damage. The outbreak of a fire in a plant producing or using chemicals can spread poisonous gases far and wide. With the growing awareness of the environmental damage that can be inflicted, companies are being forced to recognize that effective harm control is not just a matter of protecting the people inside the workplace. Worrying too is what goes out of the workplace when the job is done. What effect does the product have on the customer, and the residues out of the ventilators, up the chimneys or down the drains?

## Keeping Our Feet on the Ground

How then does the safety trainer cope with this planet-ranging responsibility? This Foreword to John Morris's handbook is not intended to give an early warning to its readers to move over to another, more comfortable discipline. The universality of the new safety training laws leaves no easy escape route. There are, fortunately, some rays of light shining through the blood and thunder of this analysis. The safety laws may range widely, but they are very firmly based. Thanks to the British contribution to the new European legislation, risk assessment has been made a universal requirement in building a safe system of work. Our 1988 Control of Substances Hazardous to Health (COSHH) Regulations have been incorporated into the European laws and extended to the treatment of all workplace risks.

This risk assessment legislation lays down a simple basic logic to the building of a safe system of work. It covers all the perspectives of hazards coming in and going out of the workplace and provides a standard framework for controlling them at all stages of their journey into, through and out of the workplace. In a single briefing, it would be impossible to go into detail on all the dimensions of health, safety and environmental policy. But this approach to the logic of risk assessment does reveal all the major perspectives of the interactive pressures on safety management, and sets out the pattern of steps to impose firm controls upon them.

The controlling steps cover three broad lines of defence against risks. First a safe system has to be built and safely operated. Secondly, it has to be effectively audited, maintained and developed to meet new demands. Thirdly, and this is where the quality assurance approach needs to be developed, firm and tested emergency procedures have to be in place to deal with break-ins, breakdowns and the breakthroughs of polluting wastes. These are illustrated in the map of risks contained in the handbook.

Understanding the principles and application of risk assessment as set out here will provide both a clear method of building a system as well as an overview of how far the system ranges. Trained managers will be able to keep in view the concerns of the workforce, the customers, the law enforcers, as well as the local and wider environment, at the same time holding their own feet firmly on the ground!

TONY CORFIELD
*National Co-ordinator,*
National Health & Safety Groups Council

# Introduction

You may be forgiven for wondering if yet another book on health and safety management is really necessary – there have certainly been a large number of words written on the subject already. Hopefully though, this book will be different for two reasons. First, it is aimed at those who, with no previous experience, suddenly find that the boss has 'promoted' them to be the company health and safety manager. Second, it has been written by someone who found himself in precisely that position, so the story starts at the beginning with no prior knowledge assumed.

Comment has been passed that the title is incomplete – The Newly Appointed what? My intention was to leave it deliberately vague. No matter what position you have been appointed to – even self-employed – there is something in this book that applies to you.

I was fortunate enough to attend a course on health and safety management at Birmingham University which was run by Tony Corfield and John Phillips on behalf of the Birmingham Health and Safety Association. I am indebted to my two tutors and have plagiarized their notes unmercifully – especially the course handbook *Safety Management* by Tony Corfield. On completion of the course my initial task was to rewrite totally the Safety Policy Statement for the Institute for Supervision and Management. This entailed the design and implementation of the forms and procedures to ensure a safe method of working. Thus, although not an expert in the health and safety field, I do at least have some practical experience of the difficulties faced by those among you who have been thrown in at the deep end.

My main objective with this book is to provide enough general information to enable the reader to formulate and maintain a health and safety policy. It would, of course, be impossible to cover every work situation so the information will necessarily be confined to those areas that are common to many occupations. More specific information may be found in the references given on page 123.

The book is divided broadly into three areas:

- *The Law.* Before attempting to formulate a health and safety policy it is obviously necessary to have an understanding of the relevant laws.
- *Implementation.* With the knowledge of what the law requires of us we can set about carrying out a risk assessment and drawing up our health and safety policy.
- *Maintenance.* Once the health and safety policy is in place it must be maintained. Successful health and safety management does not depend solely on an intimate knowledge of the rules and regulations: it needs an understanding of what motivates people. How do you persuade the boss to spend money on health and safety in a recession? How do you persuade employees that wearing the protective equipment provided is in their best interests?

Health and safety, in common with many other occupational areas, has its share of abbreviations and specialized terminology which can appear unintelligible to the uninitiated. For that reason, I have included a list of abbreviations at the start.

Although in no way wishing to denigrate the role of women in health and safety, in the interests of style and grammar – and to make it easier for the author – the male pronoun has been used throughout the text. Thus, except where the context renders it illogical, references to 'he', 'his' and 'him' can be taken as referring to both male and female.

This book may not provide all the answers but, hopefully, it will point the reader in the right direction. First, though, a word of warning. This book cannot, nor does it seek to, replace the official publications. At best, it can only provide guidelines to the mass of health and safety legislation. Neither should this book be quoted as an authoritative source of health and safety law – only the Acts and Regulations themselves can provide that.

JOHN R. MORRIS
December 1996

# List of Abbreviations

| | |
|---|---|
| ACOP | Approved Code of Practice |
| BSI | British Standards Institute |
| | |
| carcinogen | Substance which encourages the growth of cancer |
| CDM | See CONDAM |
| CHIP | Chemicals (Hazard Information and Packaging) Regulations 1993 |
| CONDAM | Construction (Design and Management) Regulations 1994 |
| COSHH | Control of Substances Hazardous to Health Regulations 1988 |
| | |
| db | Decibel |
| db(A) | Decibel adjusted for frequency |
| DSE | Display Screen Equipment |
| | |
| EC | European Commission |
| EEC | European Economic Community |
| EHO | Environmental Health Officer |
| EHSA | European Health and Safety Agency |
| EMAS | Employment Medical Advisory Service (of the HSE) |
| EPA | Environmental Protection Act 1990 |
| EU | European Union |
| | |
| FA | Factories Act 1961 |
| FPA | Fire Protection Act 1971 |
| FPR95 | Fire Precautions (Places of Work) Regulations 1995 |
| | |
| HASWA | Health and Safety at Work etc. Act 1974 |
| HAVS | Hand-arm vibration syndrome |
| hazard | Something with the potential to cause harm |
| HMP | Her Majesty's Inspectorate of Pollution |
| HMSO | Her Majesty's Stationery Office |
| HSC | Health and Safety Commission |
| HSE | Health and Safety Executive |
| HSW | Workplace (Health, Safety and Welfare) Regulations 1992 |
| Hz | Hertz |

| | |
|---|---|
| IAC | Industry Advisory Committee |
| $L_{EP,d}$ | Mathematical equation to express measurement of average noise levels over a given TWA |
| LEV | Local exhaust ventilation |
| LPG | Liquid Petroleum Gas |
| MEL | Maximum Exposure Limit |
| MHO | Manual Handling Operations Regulations 1992 |
| MHSW | Management of Health and Safety at Work Regulations 1992 |
| MOE | Means of Escape |
| OEL | Occupational Exposure Limits |
| OES | Occupational Exposure Standard |
| OSRP | Offices, Shops and Railway Premises Act 1963 |
| PAT | Portable Appliance Tester |
| PPE | Personal Protective Equipment |
| PSTGC | Pressure Systems and Transportable Gas Containers Regulations 1989 |
| PUWE | Provision and Use of Work Equipment Regulations 1992 |
| RIDDOR | Reporting of Injuries, Diseases and Dangerous Occurrences Regulations 1995 |
| risk | The likelihood that harm from a specific hazard will occur |
| SCOP | Statutory Code of Practice |
| SRSC | Safety Representatives and Safety Committee Regulations |
| SWL | Safe Working Load |
| TWA | Time Weighted Average |
| User | A person who habitually uses Display Screen Equipment as part of his normal work |
| UV | Ultra-Violet |
| VDU | Visual Display Unit |
| VWF | Vibration white finger |
| WBV | Whole body vibration |
| WC | Water closet |
| WRULD | Work related upper limb disorder |

# CHAPTER 1

# Health and Safety?

I have included this short introductory chapter because so often people will say things like:

'Health and safety? I can't afford to spend the time to worry about that!', or:

'Health and safety? There's no way I can afford to implement all those regulations!'

They are right of course. Health and safety is time consuming, and may be costly. However, the alternative may be even more time consuming, and even more costly.

The workplace may be full of expensive machinery and materials but, without people, they are virtually useless. People are a company's most valuable asset, so it makes economic sense to look after them. What's more, managers have a legal duty to protect the workforce.

The 1990 labour force survey carried out for HSC revealed the following staggering statistics of the probable cost of industrial accidents:

- there are nearly 1.5 million work-related injuries every year, of which only just over half are reportable as laid down in the definition given in RIDDOR (see Chapter 12);
- over 2 million people annually suffer from illnesses which they believe were caused or aggravated by their work;
- there are approximately 29 million days lost in industry each year due to injuries and the effects of ill health – the equivalent of one day for every person in work;
- HSE research found that, in 1988/89, the cost to the country of accidents occurring during manual handling operations was £90 million (they think this may be an underestimate!);
- further HSE research found that the cost to the country of musculo-skeletal disease among the working population exceeds £25 billion, £1.5 billion of which was caused by occupational factors.

One would think that statistics like these would be reason enough to make health and safety a high priority, but figures that large, when said quickly, lose their impact. Much more telling are the individual figures. In 1990, accidents and ill health cost businesses between £4.5 billion and £9.5 billion. This works out to between £170 and £360 for each person employed. Most of this is the uninsured cost of many small accidents which did not involve any injury, but could easily have done. Figure 1.1 shows the relationship between insured costs and uninsured costs – so, for every £1 recovered from insurance, between £8 and £36 has to be found by the employer.

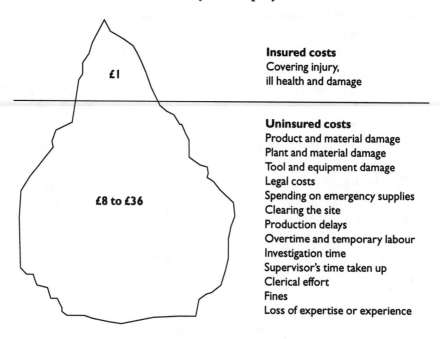

**Insured costs**
Covering injury,
ill health and damage

£1

**Uninsured costs**
Product and material damage
Plant and material damage
Tool and equipment damage
Legal costs
Spending on emergency supplies
Clearing the site
Production delays
Overtime and temporary labour
Investigation time
Supervisor's time taken up
Clerical effort
Fines
Loss of expertise or experience

£8 to £36

Figure 1.1: Relationship between insured costs and uninsured costs

Statistics show that the costs of *not* being healthy or safe are greater in the long run. For every hour not given to health and safety, there may be many hours in time lost, for example:

- by the victim;
- in investigating the incident and writing the report;
- possibly by having to console grieving loved ones;
- in dealing with the police, safety inspectors and intrusive reporters;
- in restoring the *status quo*;
- in reassuring worried employees;
- in answering questions from curious customers.

Time lost is money lost. To this could be added the cost of:

- repairing or replacing damaged machinery and equipment;
- replacing damaged or lost materials;
- lost production;
- lost orders through lost customer confidence;
- payment of sick pay;
- increased insurance premiums;
- defending prosecutions;
- paying fines;
- recruiting and training replacement staff; and so on.

Of course, another 'cost' of not taking care of health and safety needs is becoming one of the accident statistics yourself.

Perhaps the original statements should be changed to read:

'Health and safety? I can't afford not to spend the time to worry about that!'; and

'Health and safety? There's no way I can afford not to implement all those regulations!'

# CHAPTER 2

# The Law

Before any discussion on the implementation of a health and safety policy statement can begin, a knowledge of the laws relating to health and safety is needed. There are five types of law:

- Acts of Parliament
- Regulations issued under those Acts
- Approved Codes of Practice (ACOPs)
- Statutory Codes of Practice (SCOPs)
- Guidance Notes.

## Acts of Parliament

Numerous attempts were made in the nineteenth century to legislate for safety in British industry, but the laws that were passed were mainly ineffective, too narrow in their scope and unenforceable. The first real Safety Act was in 1901 which empowered the Secretary of State to issue Regulations on specific aspects of health and safety. It was not until the 1950s that any further legislation was enacted when a number of laws were passed each governing a particular industry:

- Agriculture (Poisonous Substances) Act 1952
- Mines and Quarries Act 1954
- Agriculture (Health, Safety and Welfare Provisions) Act 1956
- Factories Act 1961
- Offices, Shops and Railway Premises Act 1963 (OSRP)
- Fire Precautions Act 1971.

### Factories Act 1961

Prior to 1974, the Factories Act formed the main basis of penal law in relation to health and safety. The Act covered five main areas: health, safety, welfare, home workers and notices, returns and records. Although replaced or repealed in parts, the Factories Act will set the main standards for health and safety to be complied with in factories for some time to come.

### Offices, Shops and Railway Premises Act 1963 (OSRP)

This Act follows broadly the same principles as those found in the Factories Act but, as its name suggests, applies to different types of working environment.

### The Health and Safety at Work etc. Act 1974 (HASWA)

HASWA did not replace or repeal all the laws that went before it. The Act was evolved by the Robens Committee, which met from 1970 to 1972, to provide inspectors with the instrument to enforce earlier laws. For example, it is an offence under Section 14 of the Factories Act to remove a guard from a machine. Such a contravention, however, would be prosecuted under the relevant section of HASWA rather than the Factories Act.

### Other Acts

Other laws which stand alone include:

- Food Safety Act 1990
- Environmental Protection Act 1990.

## Regulations

The Acts themselves cannot contain every detail of how the content and context of an Act will be enacted. The Secretary of State issues Regulations under the Act which will give that detail. Regulations are instructions to industry on how to implement the requirements of the Act. They can be divided into four types:

- General in scope, e.g. Reporting of Industrial Diseases and Dangerous Occurrences Regulations 1995 (RIDDOR); Health and Safety (First Aid) Regulations 1981.
- Limited in scope, e.g. Control of Lead at Work Regulations 1980; Control of Asbestos at Work Regulations 1987.
- Functional, e.g. Electricity at Work Regulations 1989; Food Hygiene Regulations 1970.
- Industry related, e.g. Construction (Design and Management) 1994 (CONDAM); Pottery (Health and Welfare) Special Regulations 1950.

## Approved Codes of Practice (ACOPs)

Further amplification to the Regulations is given by Approved Codes of Practice. ACOPs give practical guidance as to how industry can conform with the detail of the respective Regulations. Codes of Practice are usually drawn up after wide consultation with employers, trade unions and professional bodies and become ACOPs when 'approved' by the Secretary of State.

## Statutory Codes of Practice (SCOPs)

SCOPs are similar to ACOPs but are not normally generated from industry. They are usually issued by the Health and Safety Executive (HSE) on behalf of the Health and Safety Commission (HSC), Industry Advisory Committees (IACs) or in conjunction with a body such as the British Standards Institute (BSI).

## Guidance Notes

Occasionally, Guidance Notes will be issued along with, or supplementary to, Regulations when an ACOP or SCOP is issued. Guidance Notes in booklet form may be issued by HSE, HSC, IACs or by industry itself.

## ACOP, SCOP and Guidance Status

ACOPs, SCOPs and Guidance Notes have quasi-legal status – rather like the Highway Code – in that they are not mandatory and you cannot be prosecuted for failing to comply with them. However, if failure to comply with an ACOP, SCOP or Guidance Notes should lead to a reportable incident, then that failure may be used in evidence against you.

## European Community Directives

The European Commission passes down many laws in the form of European Community (EC) Directives. These Directives are instructions to the governments of member states to implement a particular aspect of EC law and, in themselves, have no power over employers in the UK. The power comes from the fact that the UK Government issues Regulations under an appropriate Act of Parliament. Six new Regulations were issued under HASWA in 1992 as a direct result of EC Directives:

- Workplace (Health, Safety and Welfare) Regulations 1992
- Management of Health and Safety at Work Regulations 1992
- Provision and Use of Works Equipment Regulations 1992
- Health and Safety (Display Screen Equipment) Regulations 1992
- Manual Handling Operations Regulations 1992
- Personal Protective Equipment at Work Regulations 1992.

# CHAPTER 3

# The Health and Safety at Work etc. Act 1974

The Health and Safety at Work etc. Act (HASWA) is a most important piece of legislation. For the first time, virtually all employees in the UK were given statutory protection at work. Prior to this only 50 per cent of the working population were covered. All persons at work whether employers, employees or self-employed are covered with the exception of domestic servants in a private household. The Act states that everyone at work has duties and responsibilities in respect of health and safety – both employers and employees. As might be imagined, the duties imposed on employers far outweigh those on the employee but they are there nevertheless. Part I of the Act deals with health, safety and welfare in relation to work and we shall examine this in some detail. However, before examining the more important sections of the Act, it is worth taking a moment to consider the title as every word has some significance:

'*Health*': Health was specifically covered in legislation for the first time. Apart from health risks in general, the Act included such matters as mental health, stress, drugs, alcohol and smoking.

'*Safety*': The 1974 Act brought all the existing industrial safety laws together under one all-embracing statute. The Factories Act 1961, the Offices, Shops and Railway Premises Act 1963, the Mines and Quarries Act 1954, the Agriculture Acts of 1952 and 1956, *et al*, were reinforced rather than repealed by HASWA.

'*At Work*': Anyone who is 'at work' in any situation or location is covered by this law: even the travelling salesman in his company car.

'*Etc.*': This indicates that this law is an enabling piece of legislation – it is all-embracing and provides for every aspect of occupational health, safety, welfare and hygiene. It also provides for Regulations to be enacted under the Act without recourse to Parliament.

Within the Act itself, there are two phrases which reoccur with monotonous regularity:

'*It shall be the duty*': This means that it is the *duty* of every employer and employee to fulfil every aspect of the HASWA without excuse.

'*So far as is reasonably practicable*': Many saw this as a get-out clause. It isn't – rather the reverse in fact. If it is reasonable and practicable then it *must* be done. The onus is on the employer to prove that something in the interests of health and safety is not reasonable or practicable. Whilst in the normal course of British justice one is judged to be innocent until proved guilty, under HASWA you are guilty until you prove your innocence!

## Duties of Employees

Every person in a business is an employee, whatever their status in the firm. Those in positions of authority have additional health and safety responsibilities, but are still required to comply with the duties of employees set out in Sections 7 and 8 of HASWA.

### Duty to self and others
**Section 7(a):**

> 'Employees have a duty to take reasonable care for their own health, safety and welfare at work, and that of others who may be affected by their acts or omissions.'

This duty emphasises the key principle of HASWA – safety at work is everyone's business. Should an employee be injured at work, the extent to which the employee's own acts or omissions contributed to the accident will be taken into account when the question of compensation arises.

### Duty to Employers
**Section 7(b):**

> 'To co-operate with their employer in all the things which he does in order to discharge his health and safety responsibilities.'

Employees have a duty to obey the company's health and safety policy. They must wear or use any personal protective equipment provided by their employer in the interests of health, safety, welfare and hygiene. Failure to respond at once to the emergency evacuation signal, or preventing others from doing so, would also be a breach of this duty.

**Section 8:**

> 'Not intentionally or recklessly to interfere with or misuse anything provided in the interests of health, safety and welfare.'

Amongst the many breaches of this section, two are most common: High-spirited pranks such as setting off fire extinguishers when no emergency exists; and wedging open fire doors with a fire extinguisher (this would also be a breach of Section 7(a)).

## Duties of Employers

The main duties of employers are given in Sections 2, 3, 4, 5, 6 and 9 of HASWA and include:

- duties to employees (Section 2);
- duties to non-employees (Section 3);
- duties relating to premises (Section 4);
- duty to control emissions into the atmosphere (Section 5);
- duties of designers, manufacturers, importers and suppliers of substances (Section 6);
- duties concerning personal protective equipment (Section 9).

### Section 2 – Duties to Employees
It may be useful to first define the term 'Employee' for the purposes of health and safety:

- An employee is any person who is permanently or temporarily on the payroll for the purpose of PAYE and class 1 National Insurance Contributions (NIC).
- Anyone who is regularly on the premises for training and/or work experience and who is not a visitor, contractor, self-employed person or customer is to be treated as an employee.

### Section 2(1) – The General Duty

'It shall be the duty of every employer to ensure, so far as is reasonably practicable, the health, safety and welfare at work of all his employees.'

But remember, if matters go wrong, it is for the employer to show that the actions he took were reasonably practicable in all the circumstances.

The general duty in Section 2(1) is amplified by five specific requirements in Section 2(2):

### Section 2(2)(a) – Plant and Equipment

'The provision and maintenance of plant and systems of work that are, so far as is reasonably practicable, safe and without risks to health.'

All plant and equipment must be safe, without risk to health and regularly maintained. It should not be thought that this Section applies only to industry; it has considerable relevance to offices. Most offices nowadays have photocopiers and, probably, a procedure for dealing with stoppages. This is a 'system of work'. The safe operation and maintenance of lifts or central heating boilers would also be covered under this Section. In general, if there is a real risk of danger, or there is some degree of complexity or unfamiliarity with the work or some practical precautions are possible, a written safe system of work should be available. Ideally, the safe system should be developed in liaison with the workers who normally operate or maintain the equipment.

In the event of any reportable injury or dangerous occurrence concerning a piece of equipment, the visiting inspector can be expected to ask to see the written system of work fairly early in the proceedings. Many a defence argument has failed due to the lack of documentation.

### Section 2(2)(b) – Handling Materials

'Arrangements for ensuring, so far as is reasonably practicable, safety and absence of risks to health in connection with the use, handling, storage and transport of articles and substances.'

'Substance' is defined (in Section 53) as 'any natural or artificial substance, whether in solid or liquid form or in the form of a gas or vapour'. This sub-section covers all materials and articles used at work and all work activities.

## Section 2(2)(c) – Training

'The provision of such information, instruction, training and supervision as is necessary to ensure, as far as is reasonably practicable, the health and safety at work of his employees.'

It is the duty of employers to ensure compliance with the law and their company's health and safety rules. Simply saying that employees have been given a copy of the health and safety policy statement, or that they have been issued with protective clothing and told to wear it is not enough. It is an offence not to give supervision in the workplace – for this reason many firms do not allow 'lone working'. All employers have a special duty towards young people under the age of 18 years who must never be left alone in the workplace.

## Section 2(2)(d) – Safe Place of Work

'So far as is reasonably practicable as regards any place of work under the employer's control, the maintenance of it in a condition that is safe and without risks to health and the provision and maintenance of means of access to and egress from it that are safe and without such risks.'

This Section calls for a safe place in which to work. The Act specifically mentions the maintenance of buildings and safe methods of entry and exit, but also includes safe routes within the workplace.

## Section 2(2)(e) – Working Environment

'The provision and maintenance of a working environment for his employees that is, so far as is reasonably practicable, safe, without risks to health and adequate as regards facilities and arrangements for their welfare at work.'

A safe and healthy work environment requires adequate lighting, heating and ventilation in the workplace. The smoking issue, Legionnaires' Disease, sick building syndrome, and air and water quality are also covered by this sub-section.

### Section 2(3) – Health and Safety Policy

'Except in such cases as may be prescribed, it shall be the duty of every employer to prepare and as often as may be appropriate revise written statement of his general policy with respect to the health and safety at work of his employees and the organisation and arrangements for the time being in force for carrying out that policy, and to bring the statement and any revision to the notice of all his employees.'

Employers with fewer than five employees need not have a written statement of their policy on health and safety matters – although it is still a good idea to have one. There is no set format for health and safety policies, but HSC and HSE have published several booklets – some of them available free of charge – to assist in drawing up a statement.
*More assistance in:*

* Chapter 6.

### Section 2(4–7) – Safety Representatives and Safety Committees
These sub-sections provide for safety representatives and safety committees.
*More details in:*

* Safety Representatives and Safety Committees Regulations 1977.
* HSC have issued guidance on the Regulations.
* See Chapter 5 for information concerning consultation with employees.

### Section 3 – Duties to Persons Other Than Employees

'It shall be the duty of every employer to conduct his undertakings in such a way as to ensure, so far as is reasonably practicable, that persons not in his employment who may be affected thereby are not thereby exposed to risks to their health or safety.'

This Section requires employers to ensure that persons not in their employment are not adversely affected by their operations. It also applies to the self-employed. Wherever possible employers and the self-employed should inform persons that might be adversely affected by their operations of the dangers.

Non-employees fall into three categories:

- contractors carrying out work on the premises;
- business callers, e.g. representatives or customers;
- visitors.

There is, in fact, a further group who could be adversely affected by an employer's operations – those living in close proximity to the premises who may be affected by noise, smell or atmospheric pollution.

However, of the first three categories of non-employees, contractors provide the biggest problem. It is not sufficient for an employer simply to tell a contractor what the company's health and safety policy is. He must devise ways to ensure that the contractor is, in fact, complying with that policy. The term 'contractor' covers a wide variety of persons – not all obvious. Examples include:

- service engineers repairing or maintaining equipment on a client's premises;
- a floral decorator visiting to water or change plants;
- a taxi driver calling to pick up or drop off a fare;
- temporary agency staff.

Contractors tend to create greater safety problems than employees for a variety of reasons: The contractor may have been briefed on the company health and safety policy, but he may not have fully briefed his staff; the client has deadlines and wants the work done quickly, or he changes the job specification during the course of the contract; or the contractors may not be properly or constantly supervised.

For the second and third categories of non-employee there is a need to take reasonable measures to minimize danger. Examples of likely problems include:

- the factory tour during which one of the party slips away to the toilet and loses contact with the main party;
- mother bringing her new baby onto the premises to show former colleagues;
- older children brought to work either for domestic reasons or as a 'treat'.

The above situations are by no means uncommon and do pose problems for the employer. It is very difficult to take a hard line, especially in the case of older children brought into work, perhaps, while the parent voluntarily works overtime to meet a deadline. However, in the event of an accident causing injury to the child, whatever the cause, any goodwill between employer and parent is likely to evaporate quickly when the question of compensation or damages arises. In addition, as the accident occurred outside the law any claim by the employer against a policy to cover accidents at work will probably be rejected, even if children of employees were covered.

## Section 4 – Premises

This Section covers the duties of persons in charge of premises to persons who are not their employees but use premises over which they have control. The primary duty is to ensure that the premises, the means of access to and exit from them, any plant or substance in them, or provided for use there, are safe and without risk to health.

The term 'premises' is defined by Section 53 and 'includes any place and, in particular, includes any vehicle, vessel, aircraft or hovercraft; and installation on land (including the foreshore and other land intermittently covered by water), and offshore installation and any other installation (whether floating or resting on the seabed or the subsoil thereof, or resting on other land covered with water or the subsoil thereof), and any text or movable structure.'

## Section 5 – Emissions into the Atmosphere

This Section relates to emissions of noxious or offensive substances into the atmosphere. Any substances that may be emitted must be rendered harmless and ineffective. It would appear from Section 5(3) that the terms 'noxious or offensive' are not confined to the description on a label, but what is perceived by a user or third person to be noxious or offensive. Section 5(4) of the Act attributes responsibility to the person in control of the process of manufacture and not solely to the owner of the premises.

It is possible that employers doing their best to expel dust, fumes and gases from within the workplace – thus obeying Section 2(2)(e) – could breach Section 5 by polluting the external environment. Hence the need to render harmless any expelled substances.

*More assistance in:*

• Health and Safety (Emissions into the Atmosphere) Regulations 1983.

### Section 6 – Manufacturers and Suppliers

This Section places duties on persons who design, manufacture, import, supply, erect or install any article, plant, machinery, equipment or appliances for use at work, or manufacture, import or supply any substance for use at work. It also places duties for research on designers and manufacturers.

Every employer is likely to be affected by these provisions as a purchaser or user of articles or substances.

*More assistance in:*

- HSE booklet HSG 27(Rev.), Substances for use at work; the provision of information.

### Section 9 – Charge to Employees

Section 9 prohibits the levying on an employee of any charge in respect of anything done or provided in pursuance of any specific requirement of any of the legislation for health, safety and welfare.

Thus, it would be a breach of the Act if the employer were to charge for the provision of protective clothing or equipment necessary to perform their work safely. Similarly, if it is deemed necessary for employees to undergo medical examinations as a precaution, no charge may be levied for these.

### Other Sections of HASWA

There are many other Sections of HASWA which need not be detailed here. However, there are two other sections that should be mentioned:

- **Section 36.** This Section is concerned with cases where a health and safety offence is committed by one person as a consequence of the default of another. In such circumstances, that other person may be proceeded against, whether or not proceedings are taken against the first person.
- **Section 37.** 'Where an offence under any of the relevant statutory provisions committed by a body corporate is proved to have been committed with the consent or connivance of, or to have been attributable to any neglect on the part of any director, manager, secretary or other similar officer of the body corporate, or a person who was purporting to act in such capacity, he as well as the body corporate shall be liable to be proceeded against and punished accordingly.'

  Simply put, if a company commits a health and safety offence and the blame for the breach – or even the cause of it – is found to be that of a director or manager, the individual concerned may be indicted whether or not proceedings are taken against the company. It is not only the managers at the operational end of the company who could be affected by this Section. A finance director who refused to release funds for necessary safety work or equipment, for example, could be liable. In addition, if we think back to our hapless employer who allowed an employee to bring onto the premises a child who subsequently sustained an injury, he too could be indicted under this section.

# CHAPTER 4

# Enforcement

Having looked in broad terms at the health and safety laws which affect us, it might be useful, at this point, to look briefly at the question of enforcement. Summonses, convictions and the level of fines have increased considerably in recent years, but enforcement officers (usually known as inspectors) prefer to resolve problems by other means if possible. Inspectors have considerable powers as shown in Figure 4.1.

## Advice

Working on the premise that attack is the best form of defence it may be wise to seek advice before a serious situation develops. There are three enforcement authorities covering health, safety, welfare, food hygiene and fire:

- the HSE;
- local authority environmental health departments;
- local fire authorities.

It may seem like stirring a hornets' nest to call in an enforcement agency when there is no need, but they would rather help you to prevent an accident than prosecute you for having one.

## If the Inspector Calls

As can be seen from Figure 4.1, an inspector has the power to enter your premises without prior warning. If, however, the visit is planned, arrange for someone who has both authority and knowledge to escort him. Make sure that all relevant documentation is to hand:

- the master copy of the company health and safety policy;
- fire certificate and log book;

- To enter premises at reasonable times or at any time where there is danger without prior notice.
- To take a policeman with him if he feels he may be obstructed.
- To take with him any persons duly authorized by his enforcing authority and to take any equipment or material required for any purpose.
- To carry out an inspection or investigation.
- To require parts of premises to be left undisturbed for as long as is deemed necessary.
- To take measurements, photographs and recordings as necessary.
- To take samples of articles or substances found on the premises, or to sample the atmosphere in the vicinity of the premises.
- To have any article or substance dismantled or subjected to any process or test.
- To take possession of an article or substance that is necessary to facilitate an examination, to prevent tampering or to make available as evidence in proceedings.
- To require a person to give evidence and make statements.
- To inspect or take copies of relevant documents or registers.
- To require assistance as necessary.

Figure 4.1: Powers of the Inspectors

- records of statutory inspections (e.g. for lifts, cranes etc.);
- health and safety training records;
- assessments (e.g. COSHH);
- procedures for serious and imminent danger.

All inspectors are appointed in writing by the enforcing authority and are obliged to show their identity card if requested – ask to see it.

## Enforcement

If an inspector find hazards that are a risk to health, safety or welfare he will notify the company in writing suggesting action to remedy the situation. Failure to comply with the suggested action is not, in itself, an offence; however, failure to fulfil one's duty as an employer is and may lead to the issue of an enforcement notice which can take one of two forms:

- **Improvement notice.** Improvement notices are used by inspectors when, in their opinion, a business is not complying with the law and action needs to be taken. They tell an employer how and why he is contravening the law and give a date by which the problem must be remedied. If an inspector intends to issue an improvement notice the employer will have the right, on request, to a written explanation of what is wrong, an outline of what needs to be done and by when, before the notice is issued. The employer then has two weeks during which to make representations if he thinks the proposed notice should be changed or should not be issued. A fair and fresh look will then be taken at the proposed action in light of the representations. If representations are not received, the notice will be issued. An improvement notice can be appealed within 14 days of receipt. The appeal will be heard by an industrial tribunal, and no action need be taken on the notice until the outcome is known. The improvement notice is the less serious of the enforcement notices, but should not be considered non-urgent, as failure to comply is a serious offence.
- **Prohibition notice.** If either an improvement notice has not been complied with or the situation is too dangerous to permit work to continue, a prohibition notice may be issued. The inspector does not require an operation to breach a statutory provision; the sole criterion is the risk of injury. Prohibition means what it says: the operation or machine must stop until the required improvements have been made. It is possible to appeal against a prohibition notice, but the notice must be complied with pending the hearing which is also before an industrial tribunal.

An improvement or prohibition notice may be issued against a director, manager, employee, building, machine, process, material or anything affecting health, safety, welfare or hygiene. In the case of a prohibition notice against an employee there would be no option other than to transfer him to another job – or dismiss him.

## Complaints Procedure

The procedures and rights provide ways for the employer to have his views heard. If you are not happy with the inspector's action, you should let the inspector's manager know:

- *If the inspector is from the HSE.* Speak or write to the manager. He will then investigate your complaint and tell you what is going to be done about it. The HSE finds that most complaints are settled in this way, very often immediately. If you are still not satisfied you can write to the Director General of the HSE who will see that your complaint is followed up promptly and fairly. You can also write to ask your MP to take up your case with the HSE or with Ministers. Your MP may also ask the independent Parliamentary Commissioner for Administration (the Ombudsman) to review your complaint.

- *If the inspector is from the local authority.* Contact the manager and ask for the complaint to be investigated. If you are still not satisfied, contact the Chief Executive of the local authority concerned. You could also write to your local councillor. You have a right to let the HSC know if you consider that the procedure outlined has not been fulfilled, and can contact the HSE's local authority unit who will see that your complaint is followed up promptly and fairly with the local authority. If they are unable to resolve the problem, they will report the matter to the HSC. You can also make a complaint to the Local Ombudsman in England, Scotland or Wales.

---

- Failure to comply with the general duties (Sections 2–7). These are the sections covering the duties of employers, employees, persons in charge of premises, manufacturers, suppliers, and so on.

- Contravention of sections 8 or 9. These are the duties not to interfere with safety equipment, and the employer's duty not to charge for safety clothing and equipment, or for necessary medical examinations.

- Contravention of Health and Safety Regulations.

- Making a false statement.

- Making a false entry in a register.

- Obstructing an inspector.

- Preventing any persons appearing before an inspector.

- Pretending to be an inspector.

- Contravening the terms of a licence.

- Contravening an enforcement notice.

- Improperly using or disclosing information.

---

Figure 4.2: Offences under the Health & Safety at Work etc. Act 1974

## Sanctions

The HSE has indicated that, because of indifference to health and safety in many places, it intends to pursue prosecutions in the higher courts. There is also a growing trend to prosecute offences under Sections 3 and 7 of HASWA. The level of penalties imposed is determined by the circumstances and nature of the offence. Since 1992, magistrates' courts and sheriff courts in Scotland have the power to impose fines up to £20,000 for most health and safety offences, and imprisonment for up to six months for offences relating to breaches of enforcement orders. Higher courts may impose unlimited fines and imprisonment up to three years. Figure 4.2 details the offences under HASWA which could attract imprisonment or a fine, or both.

# CHAPTER 5

# Implementation

## General

Armed with the basic knowledge of what the law requires, we can now consider what you need to do to stay within the law. In the chapters which follow, the word 'must' has been used to indicate a definite legal requirement. Direct quotations from the Regulations are enclosed in quotation marks. The word 'should' indicates information taken from an ACOP or HSE Guidance so describes actions which are desirable rather than mandatory.

Basically, the law says you must:

- have a written up-to-date health and safety policy if you employ five or more people (see Chapter 6);
- carry out a risk assessment and, if you employ five or more people, record the main findings and your arrangements for health and safety (see Chapter 7);
- notify occupation of premises to your local inspector if you are a commercial or industrial business;
- display a current certificate as required by the Employers' Liability (Compulsory Insurance) Act 1969 if you employ anyone;
- display the Health and Safety Law poster where all employees can easily read it, or give out the leaflet to each employee;
- notify certain types of injuries, occupational diseases and events (see Chapter 12);
- consult any employees on matters relating to health and safety at work;
- not employ children of under school-leaving age, apart from on authorized work experience schemes, if you are an industrial undertaking.

## Consultation Rights

As a result of the Health and Safety (Consultation with Employees) Regulations 1996, employers must consult with all employees not already represented by trades union safety representatives. The Consultation Regulations apply to every size of organization irrespective of activity or status.

Consulting with employees is not the same as informing them – there is a significant difference. The provision of information is already a legal requirement under the Management Regulations. Consultation does require the provision of information to employees, but the views of employees must be listened to and considered before any decisions are taken.

The employer must, in good time:

- provide adequate information on what is proposed;
- give those affected sufficient time to express their views;
- listen to and take account of the responses.

How employees are consulted is left to the discretion of the employer. Consultations may be either directly with individual employees or indirectly through safety representatives. 'Representatives' represent an employee group and must perform certain functions in order to carry out that role. Accordingly, under the Regulations, they are conferred certain rights relating to training, pay and time off during working hours. Should a representative of employee safety be refused time off or pay allowed under the Regulations, the employer can be taken to an industrial tribunal.

## Getting Organized

Chapters 6 to 15 give detailed information on the various aspects of health and safety. What follows is intended to point employers and safety managers in the right direction initially.

The overall objective is to avoid all accidents. An accident can be defined as an unexpected and undesirable event, especially one resulting in damage, injury or death. The best way to prevent unexpected and undesirable events is by good management of health and safety.

The following is reproduced with acknowledgement to the HSE.

*Know your legal duties*

If you have people working for you, or are a supplier of goods or services, there are laws protecting those whom you might affect. Find out about the occupational safety laws which apply to you.

*Provide safe methods*

Find out about safe working methods for your industry and see what published guidance is available. Make sure everyone is aware of the correct procedures – consider displaying warning notices in workplaces or near machines, or prepare a simple checklist of local rules.

*Organize the duties*

Decide who is responsible for which safety duties, making sure that there are no overlaps or gaps, and that everyone knows their own responsibilities.

Suggested supervisor's duties might be to ensure for their section that:

- they are familiar with the company safety policy and their section's arrangements;
- employees are trained and aware of the hazards at their workplace;
- staff know where to find first-aid and fire-fighting equipment;
- supervision is available at all times, particularly for young or inexperienced workers;
- safety rules are observed and, for example, protective equipment is worn or used;
- safety devices are properly adjusted and maintained;
- machinery and equipment are frequently inspected to ensure that they are properly maintained and safe to use;
- any defects are promptly reported and rectified;
- good standards of housekeeping are maintained;
- they investigate accidents and incidents, and recommend ways of preventing recurrences.

*Prepare a safety policy*

If you have five or more employees you must have a written safety policy which sets out the organization (people and responsibilities) and arrangements (systems and procedures) for health and safety in your organization. Bring it, and any revisions, to the attention of your employees.

Make clear your commitment to high standards of health and safety. Sign and date the policy and remember to review it periodically.

### Identify the risks

Walk around the premises and look for things which are unsafe, or potentially unsafe. Learn to identify hazards and the ways of dealing with them. Ignore the trivial and concentrate on those activities which could cause serious harm. But don't just look at the obvious ones – operations such as roof work, maintenance, and transport movements (including lift trucks) cause far more deaths and serious injuries each year than many mainstream activities.

Consider who might be harmed e.g. workers, visitors, contractors, the public.

Determine the level of risk. What is the worst possible result? How likely is it to happen? How many people could be hurt if things did go wrong?

With the above information check that you are taking the right precautions to keep the main risks under control. Look at the work, talk to people and check records. Find out what actually goes on – not what you think goes on. Identify any new precautions necessary to deal with residual risks remaining in spite of your current procedures.

### Carry out a risk assessment

The previous section covered the physical side of carrying out the risk assessment. If you have five or more employees you must record the main findings (it may be a good idea to do this even if you have fewer employees).

### Train your staff

Give employees information and training so that they know and understand the arrangements for handling particular hazards. Sometimes formal training in health and safety will be necessary. Start with supervisors who have responsibility for work methods and job instruction. Use safety checklists as a guide in training.

Specific training requirements apply to some activities, for example young people using certain machines. Remember that proper training and supervision is particularly important for all young people because they may not recognize the dangers.

### Check your performance

Having set the standards for your firm, check that the rules are being followed and monitor how well you are doing. Inspections can be informal, say by a supervisor at the beginning of a working day, or formal – say once a quarter. Use checklists or notes to make sure that you don't miss important points. Look for information which will help you evaluate hazards and make improvements.

Don't forget to check for the expected improvements at the next inspection.

*Organize your information*

Keep your safety information separately organized and filed. Don't let information – like letters from your local inspector, insurance company reports, and safety and health information from suppliers – go astray. Use it to check that you are operating to the highest standards and that your safety policy is up-to-date.

*Investigate when things go wrong*

Investigation of accidents, dangerous occurrences and 'near-misses' helps to prevent recurrences. Don't investigate to attribute blame; concentrate on analyzing the facts so that you can make sensible decisions about remedial action. Incidents rarely have a single cause – usually they result from a combination of actions, errors or failures of people and equipment.

*Prepare your 'Safety Improvement Plan'*

If you find that changes are needed, decide on your priorities and how they are going to be dealt with.

- *Identify* the problem.
- *Evaluate* alternative solutions.
- *Select* appropriate action.
- *Plan* how to tackle the job.
- *Programme* the resources – people, time and money.
- *Implement* the improvement.
- *Monitor* the results.
- *Review* its effectiveness.

*Maintain interest*

You need the co-operation and active commitment of supervisors and all employees. Draw on their ideas and experience through regular health and safety meetings and briefings. If safety representatives have been appointed by trade unions you recognize, you must consult them. Encourage employees by regular review of safety reports and staff suggestions. Use posters, safety committees, and displays of safety performance.

# CHAPTER 6

# Health and Safety Policy Statement

Employers with five or more employees are legally required to provide a written health and safety policy statement that is regularly updated. This should be a statement specific to the company, setting out the general policy for protecting the health and safety of the employees, and the organization and arrangements for putting the policy into practice. The statement is important because it is the company's basic action plan on health and safety which all employees should read, understand and follow. The legal requirement aside, a safety policy statement can bring real benefits. If it is well thought out, has the employer's backing, commands respect and is thoroughly put into practice, it should lead to better standards of health and safety. Managers and employees will see the importance of the policy and will be encouraged to co-operate.

The statement should include environmental control as well as health and safety. Both big and small employers are likely to be affected by the environmental responsibilities legally imposed upon them, if only over the treatment of waste and the control of noise, odours and dust which could offend the public.

Customers, clients and main contractors as well as safety representatives or inspectors may wish to see the policy statement. They will require sufficient evidence to establish that the key points of safety management and control are covered, and that they have not been copied from a handout. The emphasis must be on thoroughness and brevity – an encyclopaedia is not required.

Under Section 2(3) of HASWA the written statement must:

- state the company's general policy on health and safety;
- describe the organization and arrangements for carrying out the policy;
- be brought to the notice of all employees;
- be revised whenever appropriate, and every revision must be brought to the attention of all employees.

Appendix B contains an example of a company health and safety policy statement. The content of each section is considered in turn below.

## Introduction

It is sufficient to give the company name and address, and the title 'Health and Safety Policy Statement'. The impression it makes will be helped if it is smartly and professionally presented.

## Objectives

This section provides an opportunity to outline, briefly, what the company makes, its size and composition, and what it is in business for. Then, its general strategy for safety, health and environmental protection can be outlined in a realistic context. Giving a brief description of this broad strategy should not be difficult. Many companies have special problems. Small firms, especially those engaged on contract, are likely to be working in unfamiliar situations. Others may have fire or chemical hazards. Suppliers may wish to show to their customers their concern for high standards of hygiene. All these can refer to their particular problems and opportunities as the focal point of their strategy.

## Organization

The Organization section has two parts. The first sets out the various grades of the people who manage, or help manage, and the second their areas of responsibility for operating and maintaining a safe system of work.

The people who manage:

- **Top and all other grades of management.** The law imposes the overriding responsibility upon the employer. So, top management is involved, but other managers must also co-operate in the safety policy. Accidents adversely affect finance, public and customer relations, employee morale, the environment and the company's legal standing. Supervisors have to ensure that the risk controls are actually applied.
- **Competent persons.** Periodic tests and examinations must be carried out by a 'competent person'. A competent person is someone who has the necessary technical expertise, training and experience to carry out the examination or test. This could be an outside organization such as an

insurance company or other inspecting organization, a self-employed person or one of the company's staff who is capable of doing the task.

- **Employees.** All employees have management responsibilities in health and safety, too. Legal duties for them to co-operate with the employer are laid down in HASWA.
- **Contractors and their staff.** Contractors must be able to control the safe conduct of their own staff at work. They must conform to the overall safety policy of the client or main contractor.
- **Safety representatives.** Where safety representatives are appointed, they have the legal right to carry out safety audits and accident investigations, and to raise and submit safety complaints for consideration by the employer. Safety representatives have a recognized place in the safety management team.

The second part of the Organization section sets out the areas of responsibility of the people listed in the first part. These are:

- **Operating a safe system of work.** The operation of a safe system of work involves the following issues:
  - the production of the health and safety policy statement, and the arrangements for its publication, maintenance and review;
  - the production of the general and other statutory risk assessments upon which the policy will be built. These need only to be referred to in the main policy statement. The full records can be added as appendices;
  - the responsibility for applying the risk removal or controls identified in the assessments. They should cover health and the environment as well as safety;
  - details of any personal protective equipment included in the controls. In small businesses working on contract, this may represent a central element in its controls;
  - those safety measures that have to be co-ordinated with clients and contractors to integrate their staffs into the whole system;
  - the organization of any technical assistance required to identify and measure certain risks beyond the scope of the people who manage.
- **Maintaining a safe system.** The system as a whole has to be checked regularly to ensure full effectiveness. This involves:
  - inspections and audits of the safe working standards of people and equipment, and of records, rules, procedures and processes;
  - official reports of accidents, investigations, injuries, equipment tests etc.;

– establishing effective employee reporting of hazards and system failures, including near-misses;

– health surveillance, where required.

- **Applying emergency procedures in the event of breakdown.** This third line of defence against occupational risks requires effective emergency procedures to be in place should the system fail for any reason. Two major areas of risk for small businesses are:

  – *Accidents and injuries.* Establish the procedures, provide notices and equipment and detail the training to be given to employees;

  – *Fire.* Establish the procedures and outline the equipment and training provided. If required, appoint emergency evacuation leaders to deal with emergencies.

The preceding analysis of the management responsibilities to be included in a safety policy is not all-inclusive. Unusual risks may be encountered, like organized robbery in places handling large amounts of cash. Problems may arise from the misreading of safety notices where non-literate workers or those for whom English is not their first language are employed. To cope with these and other such risks, special controls and staffing not spelt out in these notes may be needed.

## Arrangements

This section describes how the management responsibilities set out in the section on organization are implemented. Instruction, information and training are three clearly related modes of management and provide a convenient division for the Arrangements section. Information is a major constituent of all three modes so, inevitably, the divisions overlap. Briefing sessions, for example, can be used for conveying instructions, providing general information and training for specific skills. The majority of management responsibilities are likely to fall within the instruction section. Since safety is a legal requirement it fits neatly into this classification. Control procedures, once worked out, are binding on everyone involved – management and employees.

The other modes of presenting safety rules and procedures have their place. Decisions on controls in some cases, as for example on load handling or with visual display equipment, are improved when the experience of the operatives can be drawn upon. Information upwards, as well as downwards, has its role here. Similarly, training has a key role in some circumstances. Competence in operating emergency procedures, which occur only at rare intervals, can only be gained by prior training.

It must be borne in mind that the entries in this section have between them to incorporate all the relevant items of responsibility mentioned in the Organization section.

- **Instructions.** The first of this section's three divisions relates to instructions. In this could be included:
  - *Safety briefings.* One-off sessions to warn about a suddenly revealed hazard, for example.
  - *Health and safety policy statement.* The statement's location, availability and means of amendment could be referred to.
  - *General assessment of risks.* As above, with its possible inclusion as an appendix.
  - *Safety notices and placards.* Possible emphasis on reporting defacements or damage, and the legal duty to observe their message.
- **Information.** In the information division could be included:
  - *Safety posters, notices and journals.* These are means of stimulating interest and commitment to safety. They are often supplemented by the large range of free leaflets issued by the HSE and other bodies.
  - *Pocket safety codes for employees.* Issued by some employers and trade associations, these provide a personal guide to emergency action and other key procedures.
  - *Consultation* (information upwards). Many companies set up safety committees to draw on the experience of their employees. They are also aware of the motivating effect that consultation can generate. There are other less formal methods, like incident reporting forms and safety suggestion schemes to promote participation.
  - *Official records.* These provide reports of accident investigations, injuries, first-aid treatment, records of plant inspections, responsible persons etc.
- **Training.** Included in the training division could be:
  - *Awareness of load handling techniques and safety limits.* This is specifically required under the recent Regulations.
  - *Fire fighting and escape procedures.* In some hazardous workplaces, training in these matters is a legal requirement. It is also advisable to impart some knowledge of the nature of fire to employees to enable them to act responsibly in handling flammable material, and to react calmly and correctly in the event of fire.
  - *General safety training.* The 1992 Management of Health and Safety at Work Regulations require wide-ranging training in health and safety for employees. This could include briefing sessions on the safety arrangements in a new work situation.

The purpose of the Arrangements section is to explain the means by which the relevant policies and controls are fulfilled. There is no need to write at length on these explanations. As a general rule, just enough is necessary to show that there is substance in the general assertions being made. One of the objects of the section is to provide checkable evidence that genuine issues, real equipment and living people are being described, not extracts from textbooks.

Whilst no safety responsibility can be neglected, there may be some areas of the Arrangements section in which clients, customers and inspectors may be particularly interested. For small contractors two aspects are likely to come under observation. One is the auditing of equipment in terms of its physical condition and the competence of the operative using it. Main contractors may seek assurance that these are regularly and properly monitored. The other area of interest is the thoroughness of operative briefing. On the arrangements for these two activities, therefore, it is particularly important that the evidence in the policy statement should be clear and convincing. For food handlers, hygiene will come under close scrutiny.

## Conclusion

The policy statement needs to be completed with the signature of the chief executive on behalf of the employer (or, in the case of a partnership, by each of the partners), his status in the company, and the date when the policy was last examined and revised. An undated statement raises the suspicion that the policy has been marooned in a cupboard for some years!

### Further reading

HSE: Writing a safety policy statement: advice to employers, HSC6.

# CHAPTER 7

# Risk Assessment

## What is a Risk Assessment?

Regulation 3 of the Management of Health and Safety at Work Regulations 1992 requires all employers and self-employed persons to assess the risks to workers and any others who may be affected by the undertaking. Employers with five or more employees must also record the significant findings of that assessment.

A risk assessment should identify the hazards present in any undertaking and the extent of the risks involved. The terminology used is as follows:

- A hazard is something with the potential to cause harm (this can include substances, machines, methods of work and people).
- Risk expresses the likelihood that harm from a specific hazard will occur.
- The extent of the risk suggests the number of people who may be affected by it.

Risk, therefore, reflects both the likelihood that harm will occur and its severity. The following is taken from the HSE publication *Essentials of Health & Safety at Work*:

'As an example, think about a can of solvent on a shelf. There is a hazard if the solvent is toxic or flammable, but very little risk. The risk increases when it is taken down and poured into a bucket. Harmful vapour is given off and there is danger of spillage. Things are made much worse if a mop is then used to spread it over the floor for cleaning. The chance of harm, i.e. the risk, is then high.'

Implicit in this example is the risk of persons slipping on a wet floor – a hazard unconnected with the toxicity of the substance.

To decide what level of risk exists, consider:

- What the worst result might be. Is it a broken finger, permanent lung damage or death? The hazards given in Chapters 8 to 13 may help in this.
- How likely it is to happen. How often do you do the job? How close do people get to the hazard? How likely is it that something can go wrong?
- How many people could get hurt if things do go wrong? Could this include people who do not work for you?

## Undertaking the Assessment

There are no fixed rules about how a risk assessment should be undertaken, but the process needs to be practical. It should involve management whether or not external consultants or advisers are called in. The ACOP issued under the Regulations gives the following general principles.

- Ensure that all relevant risks or hazards are addressed:
  - First identify all hazards in the workplace. Applicable Acts or Regulations may help to identify the hazards.
  - Assess the risks from the identified hazards (remember: if there is no hazard, there is no risk!). Some risks may already be controlled in some way and the effectiveness of these controls needs to be considered when assessing the residual risk. (The residual risk is that risk remaining after the action identified to remove or control the significant risk has been taken.)
  - Decide the level of each risk:
    High risk – possible serious injury or death.
    Medium risk – minor injuries may result.
    Low risk – the likelihood of injury is negligible.
  - Be systematic in looking at hazards and risks; it may be necessary to consider them in groups, e.g. machinery, transport, substances, electrics etc., or by operations, e.g. production, administration, despatch etc.
  - Ensure all aspects of the work activity are reviewed.
- Consider what actually happens in the workplace:
  - Are the laid-down procedures being followed?
  - Are there any non-routine operations that may cause risks, e.g. maintenance, loading and off-loading, interruptions to operations, changing production schedules etc?
- Ensure that all groups of employees and others who might be affected are considered:

- Don't forget the office staff, night cleaners, maintenance staff, security personnel and visitors.
- Identify groups of workers who may be particularly at risk:
  - e.g. young or inexperienced workers, those who work alone or disabled staff.
- Take account of existing precautionary or preventive measures:
  - Are they working properly?
  - Does action need to be taken to ensure that they are properly maintained?

Figure 7.1 gives a framework checklist for a general workplace assessment. If used, a separate form should be raised for each risk.

## Sources of Advice

There are various sources of advice available to help in the task of identifying hazards and risks:

- the company's own record of accidents, near-misses and outbreaks of ill-health can provide authentic and reliable evidence of the origin, nature and intensity of risks;
- trade association and company manuals give the procedures to be followed to maintain a safe system of work;
- safety magazines have useful articles, and advertise safety products and services;
- in many cases, suppliers and manufacturers are legally required to provide health and safety data sheets for any substances, machinery or equipment they sell for use in employment. Often, safety information can be found on container labels;
- for the small business, perhaps the best source of warning about where and what hazards can be expected is the HSE's catalogue of leaflets (many available free of charge). The relevant ones are given in the References section on page 123, and also in the appropriate place in Chapters 8 to 13. A publication that I can recommend is the HSE's *Essentials of Health and Safety at Work* which provides most information under one cover. HSC publishes a newsletter about new HSE publications, changes in the law and similar items of interest. The addresses of HSC and local HSE offices are in Appendix A.

## ANALYSIS OF RISKS

| Nature of risk | People at risk |
|---|---|
| *Harmful substances/conditions* | *Employees* |
| Harmful substances | Operatives |
| Movement | Office staff |
| Noise | Cleaners |
| Stress | Catering staff |
| Errant people | Maintenance |
| Power | Lone workers |
| *Location of risk* | Drivers |
| Storage | *Other people* |
| Handling | Visitors |
| Processing | Members of public |
| Disposal | Contractors |
| *Legal standards and guidance* | Delivery & despatch staff |
| | *Specially vulnerable people* |
| | Disabled etc. |
| | Trainees |

| Precautions already taken | Changes necessary |
|---|---|
| *Correct risk treatment* | |
| Removal | Technical advice needed |
| Isolated by engineering | New or changed materials |
| Protection of human organs | New or changed working practices |
| Hygiene | Changes in management system |
| Waste disposal | Information, instruction, training |
| *Management – appropriate systems* | Communications |
| Effective controls | Auditing and monitoring |
| Properly handled | Emergency procedures & equipment |
| Adequately supervised | |
| Regularly maintained | |
| Emergency back-up: | |
|    Fire | |
|    Injury | |
|    Environment | |
| *Management infrastructure* | |
| Effective information, training, instruction | |
| Individual duty of care to report hazards: | |
|    In personal work | |
|    Observed generally | |

Figure 7.1: 'Framework' checklist for the General Workplace Risk Assessment

## Carrying out the Assessment

The amount of detail required in a risk assessment should be broadly proportionate to the risk. The purpose is not to catalogue every trivial hazard, but small things in themselves can cause big trouble. For instance, accumulations of dust and fibres around machinery frequently fuel major fires and explosions. A first rough risk assessment may be required to determine particular areas of risk. Then deal with each risk area, detailing first those risks covered by legislation, e.g. COSHH Regulations, and then the other areas not covered by legislation. If specific risk assessments have been separately carried out, such as COSHH or Fire, they do not need to be reassessed. However, the general assessment must cover all risks so cross-referencing may be necessary.

In attempting to classify risks for their presentation in the general workplace assessment, it is important to be aware that they rarely have a single origin. For example, let's assume that a brick falls off a scaffold and hits a worker on the head. The force of gravity is to blame. However, someone on the scaffold is likely to have done something to send the brick on its way. Someone else, in authority, may not have ensured that toe-boards were fixed to the scaffold to prevent the brick from being pushed off. Finally, the unfortunate recipient of the brick may have failed to observe the law by not wearing a safety helmet in a hazardous area. So, not only is more than one source of risk involved, but some of the causes are linked in a chain of cause and effect starting from defective management and ending with a law-breaking employee. Assessors should also remain alert for the unexpected; hazards may creep up from the sewers, fly in through the window, or arrive by post.

To assist in the identification of hazards, Tony Corfield in his *Guide for Small Businesses*, has produced a list of the commonly-met areas likely to produce significant risks (Figure 7.2). It is not intended to be a complete list of all the hazards that could be encountered and there will certainly be others in specialized areas.

## Recording the Assessment

There is no set layout for recording a risk assessment, but entries should be brief and to the point. A suggested layout is given in Figure 7.3 (page 40) and covers the following headings:

| Hazardous substances | Powered tools and machinery |
|---|---|
| Solvents | Abrasive wheels |
| Acids/alkalis | Power presses |
| Flammables/explosives | Air operated tools |
| LPGs | Electrical hand tools |
| Epoxy resins | Hoists/lifting equipment |
| Asbestos | Machine guarding |
| Lead compounds | Power: |
| Mineral oils/greases |   Steam |
| Atmospheric emissions |   Electrical |
| Dusts |   Radioactive |
| Hazardous wastes |   Air pressure |
| | Display screen workstations |
| **Working environment** | |
| Work at heights/depths | **Controls** |
| Ladders/scaffolding | Management procedures |
| Lift trucks | Supervision |
| Movement: | Information/training |
|   Vehicles | Monitoring – inspections/audits |
|   Tools | Consultation |
|   People | Health checks |
| Movement (obstructed etc.): | Injury records etc. |
|   Entrances/exits | Emergency procedures |
|   Passages | |
|   Climbing/descending | **People** |
| Manual handling | Employees' special needs: |
| Space: |   Disabled |
|   Congested |   New recruits |
|   Untidy, dirty |   Trainees |
|   Slippery etc. | Customers and visitors: |
|   Confined |   Violence/vandalism |
| Heat/cold |   Theft |
| Humidity | Security losses: |
| Noise |   From staff/others |
| Lighting | Employee – lapses |
| Vibration | Contractors |
| Hygiene | |

Figure 7.2: Likely hazard areas

- *Significant risk.* The ACOP to the Regulations defines a significant risk as 'non-trivial' in one place and 'serious' in another. In practice, it is probably better to err on the safe side and include the risk if any doubt exists.
- *Legal guidance.* If possible, cross-refer the risk to the Regulation which identifies the hazard.
- *Action to prevent or control the risk:*
  - existing: list the actions in force to control the risk;
  - proposed: detail the action proposed to control any uncontrolled risks remaining despite the existing actions, if any, given above.

| Significant risk | Legal guidance | Action to prevent or control | Specialists needed | People affected | Training information |
|---|---|---|---|---|---|
| | | | | | |

Assessor:                    Date:                    Page:        of:

Figure 7.3: General workplace assessment: record sheet

- *Specialists.* Are specialists required to implement any proposed action or to ensure that existing action is fully implemented?
- *People affected.* What is the extent of the risk?
- *Training information.* What training information is available for and given to employees?

A page taken from a risk assessment can be found in Figure 7.4 (page 42).

## Precautions against risks

As part of the assessment, the Regulations require us to take precautions against the significant risks recorded. These should be taken in the following priority:

- **Elimination of risk.** The first priority of management should be to eliminate the risk entirely by:
  - tackling hazards at source by applying remedial measures, e.g. by using alternative substances;
  - complete enclosure of hazardous substances;
  - guarding against hazards by, for example, treating slippery surfaces.
- **Adaptation.** If elimination is not reasonably practicable, it may be possible to adjust the job to the worker by means of engineering controls. This includes the selection and adaptation of work equipment and work methods. Full advantage should be taken of any technological progress which may reduce the risk.
- **Protection.** If neither of the above are reasonably practicable, protection against the risk must be given by the provision of personal protective equipment (PPE).

The ACOP suggests that priority should be given 'to those measures which protect the whole workplace and all those who work there'. However, it may be more appropriate to give priority action to those areas where the greatest benefit can be achieved in the shortest time. For example, there may be a small working group at serious and potentially costly risk to a particular hazard.

*Further reading*
HSE: Five steps to risk assessment, IND(G)163(L).

| Significant risk | Legal guidance | Action to prevent or control | Specialists needed | People affected | Training information |
|---|---|---|---|---|---|
| Display screen equipment | DSE Regs 1992 | | | | |
| VDU workstations in general | | All workstations have a Workstation Record raised and completed by the Health & Safety representative. In addition, the normal user of each workstation completes a Workstation User Checklist. Any problems identified are then rectified. | | All VDU users | |
| Personal protective equipment | PPE at Work Regs 1992 | | | | |
| Chemical and ink splashes in print-room | | Printroom operators are issued with overalls and gloves. | | Print-room operators | |
| Cleanliness and waste materials | HSW Reg. 9 | | | | |
| Toilets – washable floors may be slippery when wet | | Cleaners have instructions only to clean floors after all staff have vacated the building. | | All staff | |
| Office waste | | All office waste bins are emptied each evening and the waste bagged and deposited in a cov-ered skip positioned away from the building. The skip is emptied weekly by the local council. | | | |
| Fluorescent tubes | | Unserviceable fluorescent tubes are left unbro-ken by the skip for removal by the council. | Yes (for removal) | | |

Assessor: ⟨signature⟩     Date: 24 Apr 96     Page: 3 of: 8

Figure 7.4: General workplace assessment: record sheet completed

# CHAPTER 8

# The Workplace

## A Safe Place of Work

There can be many dangers at work. Safety hazards include slips, trips and falls, and fire. Health hazards include poor ventilation, lighting and seating. However, a large number of hazards are overlooked simply because they are so familiar. Not only should the movable objects, like machinery or hazardous substances, be taken into account but the immovable ones too. Floors, doors, windows, walls and ceilings – all taken for granted in the daily routine – can also deteriorate to the point where they present hazards with risk of injury.

The full requirements for workplaces are to be found in the Workplace (Health, Safety and Welfare) Regulations 1992 (HSW). They can be considered under various headings.

## Maintenance (Regulation 5)

The workplace and its equipment, devices and systems must be maintained (including cleaned if appropriate) in an efficient state, in efficient working order and in good repair. 'Efficient' in this context means efficient from the view of health, safety and welfare, not from a productivity or economical aspect.

If a potentially dangerous defect is discovered, the defect should be rectified immediately or steps taken to protect anyone who might be put at risk. Where the defect does not pose a danger but makes the equipment unsuitable for use, for example a sanitary convenience with a defective flushing mechanism, it may be taken out of service until it is repaired or replaced.

Regulation 5 of the HSW Regulations requires a system of maintenance where appropriate, for certain equipment and devices and for ventilation systems. A suitable system of maintenance involves ensuring that:

- regular maintenance (including, as necessary, inspection, testing, adjustment, lubrication and cleaning) is carried out at suitable intervals;
- any potentially dangerous defects are remedied, and that access to defective equipment is prevented in the meantime;
- regular maintenance and remedial work is carried out properly; and
- a suitable record is kept to ensure that the system is properly implemented and to assist in validating maintenance programmes.

Examples of equipment and devices which require a system of maintenance include emergency lighting, fencing, fixed equipment used for window cleaning, anchorage points used for safety harnesses, devices to limit the opening of windows, powered doors, escalators and moving walkways.

The frequency of regular maintenance, and precisely what it involves, will depend on the equipment or device concerned. The likelihood of defects developing and the foreseeable consequences, are highly relevant. The age and condition of equipment, how it is used and how often it is used should also be taken into account. Sources of advice include published HSE guidance, British and EC standards and other authoritative guidance, manufacturers' information and instructions, and trade literature.

### Further reading
BSI: Guide to building maintenance management, BS8210.
Chartered Institute of Building Services Engineers: Maintenance management for building services, TM17.


## Ventilation (Regulation 6)

Enclosed workplaces must be sufficiently well ventilated so that stale air, and air which is hot or humid because of the equipment or processes in the workplace, is replaced at a reasonable rate. The air which is introduced must, as far as possible, be free of any impurity which is likely to be offensive or cause ill-health. Air which is taken from the outside can normally be considered 'fresh', but air inlets for ventilation systems should not be sited where they may draw in contaminated air: close to a vehicle manoeuvring area, for example.

### Further reading
HSE: Ventilation of the Workplace, EH 22(Rev.).
HSE: Measurement of air change rates in factories and offices, MDHS 73.

## Temperature (Regulation 7)

The temperature in workrooms must provide reasonable comfort without the need for special clothing. Where such a temperature is impracticable because of hot or cold processes, all reasonable steps should be taken to achieve a temperature which is as close as possible to comfortable by using local heating or cooling as appropriate. The precise temperature which can be considered 'comfortable' will depend on such factors as air movement, relative humidity or even on the individual worker's metabolism. However, as a guideline workroom temperatures should be at least 16°C unless much of the work involves severe physical effort in which case the temperature can be reduced to 13°C. The temperature should be measured using an ordinary dry bulb thermometer situated close to the workstations at working height, but away from windows and radiators. It is, perhaps, worth noting that the Regulations do not specify a maximum temperature.

If fixed heating systems are used, they must be installed and maintained in such a way as to ensure that injurious or offensive fumes do not enter the workplace. Particular care should be taken with portable paraffin or liquefied petroleum gas heaters.

Sufficient thermometers must be provided to enable persons at work to determine the temperature in any workplace inside a building, but need not be provided in every workroom.

## Lighting (Regulation 8)

Every workplace must have suitable and sufficient lighting to enable people to work, use facilities and move from place to place safely without experiencing eye strain. Stairs should be well lit in such a way that shadows are not cast over the main part of the treads. Where necessary, local lighting should be provided at individual workstations, and at places of particular risk, such as pedestrian crossing points on vehicular traffic routes. Natural light must be used where practicable and workstations should be positioned so as to take advantage of the available natural light.

Lights should be repaired, replaced or cleaned as necessary before the level of lighting becomes insufficient. It is particularly important to replace flickering fluorescent tubes – especially as the strobe effect can make rotating machinery appear to be stationary.

Emergency lighting need only be provided in workrooms where sudden loss of light would present a serious risk. If installed, such lighting must be powered by a source independent of that for the normal lighting, and must operate automatically, without manual intervention, when the normal lighting fails.

*Further reading*
Electricity at Work Regulations 1989.
HSE: Lighting at Work, HS(G)38.

## Cleanliness (Regulation 9)

'Every workplace and the furniture, furnishings and fittings therein must be kept sufficiently clean.' The standard of cleanliness required will depend on the use to which the workplace is put. For example, an area where workers take their meals would be expected to be cleaner than a factory floor, and a factory floor would be expected to be cleaner than an animal house. Floors and indoor traffic routes should be cleaned at least once a week. Interior walls, ceilings and work surfaces should be cleaned at suitable intervals. Except in parts which are normally visited only for short periods, or where any soiling is likely to be light, ceilings and interior walls must be painted, tiled or otherwise treated so that they can be kept clean, and the surface treatment should be renewed when it can no longer be cleaned properly.

Cleaning should be carried out by an effective and suitable method and without creating, or exposing anyone to, a health or safety risk. This Regulation does not apply to parts of the workplace which cannot be safely reached using a 5-metre ladder.

So far as is reasonably practicable, waste material must not be allowed to accumulate in a workplace except in suitable receptacles. In factories and other workplaces of a type where dirt and refuse accumulates, any dirt and refuse which is not in suitable receptacles should be removed at least daily.

## Room Dimensions and Space (Regulation 10)

Every room where people work must have sufficient floor area, height and unoccupied space for the purposes of health, safety and welfare. Workrooms should have enough space to allow people to get to and from workstations and to move within the room with ease. The number of people who may work in any particular room at any one time will depend not only on the size of the room, but on the space taken up by furniture, fittings and equipment, and on the layout of the room. Workrooms, except those where people work for only short periods, should be of sufficient height over most of the room to enable safe access to workstations. In older buildings with obstructions, such as low beams, the obstructions should be clearly marked.

The total volume of a room when empty divided by the number of people normally working in it should be at least 11 cubic metres. In making this calculation, a room, or part of a room, which is more than 3 metres high should be counted as 3 metres high. The figure of 11 cubic metres per person is a minimum and may be insufficient if much of the room is taken up by furniture etc.

The figure of 11 cubic metres does not apply to:

- retail sales kiosks, attendant's shelters or similar small structures, or
- rooms being used for lectures, meetings or similar purposes.

## Workstations and Seating (Regulation 11)

'Every workstation must be so arranged that it is suitable both for any person at work in the workplace who is likely to work at that workstation and for any work of the undertaking which is likely to be done there.'

Workstations should be arranged so that each task can be carried out safely and comfortably. The worker should be at a suitable height in relation to the worksurface. Work materials and frequently used equipment or controls should be within easy reach without undue bending or stretching. Workstations, including seating and access to workstations, should be suitable for any special needs of the individual worker including those with disabilities. Each workstation should allow any person who is likely to work there adequate freedom of movement and the ability to stand upright. Spells of work which unavoidably have to be carried out in cramped conditions should be kept as short as possible and there should be sufficient space nearby to relieve discomfort. There should be sufficient clear and unobstructed space at each workstation to enable the work to be done safely.

Seating provided in accordance with this Regulation should where possible provide adequate support for the lower back. A footrest should be provided for any worker who cannot comfortably place his or her feet flat on the floor.

*Further reading*
HSE: Seating at Work, HS(G)57.
HSE: Ergonomics at Work, IND(G)90L.

## Display Screen Equipment

Workers using visual display units (VDUs) need well-designed work areas with suitable lighting and comfortable, adjustable seating. This helps to reduce eye strain, headaches and back or upper limb problems. No special precautions are necessary against radiation.

For habitual users the employer must:

- assess display screen workstations and reduce risks;
- plan so that there are breaks or changes of activity;
- train and inform display screen users about the health and safety aspects of their work;
- provide eye tests for users on request and at regular intervals afterwards, and special spectacles where recommended by an optometrist.

Examples of a locally designed VDU User Record, Workstation Record and Workstation User Checklist can be seen in Figures 8.1, 8.2 and 8.3 respectively.

The Health and Safety (Display Screen Equipment) Regulations 1992 give full details.

*Further reading*
HSE: Working with VDUs, IND(G)36(L) (Rev.).

## Condition of Floors and Traffic Routes (Regulation 12)

Floors and traffic routes should be of sound construction, and should have adequate strength and stability taking into account the loads placed on them and the traffic passing over them. Floors should not be overloaded.

The surfaces of floors and traffic routes should be free from any hole, slope or uneven or slippery surface which is likely to: cause a person to slip, trip or fall; cause a person to drop or lose control of anything being lifted or carried; or cause instability or loss of control of vehicles and/or their loads.

Holes, bumps or uneven areas resulting from damage or wear and tear, which may cause a person to trip or fall, should be made good. Until they can be made good, adequate precautions should be taken against accidents, for example by barriers or conspicuous marking. Temporary holes should be adequately guarded. Account should be taken of the problems faced by people with impaired or no sight.

Name:

Department:

---

## JOB SPECIFICATION

Average number of hours worked daily on a computer:

Are periodic breaks/non-computer tasks given:    YES/NO

---

## EYE CARE

Eye examination voucher no.

Signed:                                              Date:

VDU spectacles voucher no.

Signed:                                              Date

---

## TRAINING

Was training given for computers you normally use:    YES/NO

---

## HEALTH AND SAFETY

Are you aware of the ISM Health and Safety Policy:    YES/NO
(as shown in the Staff Manual)

Are you aware of the action to be taken in the event of fire:    YES/NO

Have you taken part in a Practice Emergency Evacuation:    YES/NO

Figure 8.1: VDU user record

Reference number:

Location:

Equipment provided:

    Hardware:

    Software:

    Peripherals:

_____

Last checked by Health and Safety Representative:

User Checklist completed:    YES/NO          Date:

_____

Specify any failures to meet minimum requirements and remedial action taken:

_____

Maintenance contract:

Company:

Number:                  Renewal date:

Figure 8.2: Workstation record

User name:

Workstation reference number:

---

1.  Is there sufficient room at the workstation to:
    (a)  arrange all necessary items in orderly fashion              YES/NO
    (b)  vary the position of the display and keyboard to get comfortable  YES/NO

2.  Can your chair be easily adjusted to give a comfortable and
    suitable posture?                                                YES/NO

3.  Do your legs fit comfortably beneath the desk?                   YES/NO

4.  Is the screen clear, clean, easy to read and steady with no flickering?  YES/NO

5.  Is the display free from reflections of light and windows, and is your
    field of view behind the screen free from bright lights?         YES/NO

6.  Is the workstation safe, i.e. are cables in good condition and neatly
    stowed; covers unbroken and secure; surroundings tidy; furniture
    in good repair with no sharp edges?                              YES/NO

7.  Is the environment acceptable, i.e. temperature, humidity, ventilation,
    noise and other ambient conditions?                              YES/NO

---

If the answer to any of the above questions is 'NO' then please give details here (continue overleaf if necessary):

---

Signature:                                    Date:

Figure 8.3: Workstation user checklist

Surfaces of floors and traffic routes which are likely to get wet or to be subject to spillage should be of a type which does not become unduly slippery. A slip-resistant coating should be applied where necessary. Floors surrounding machinery which could cause injury if anyone were to fall against it should be slip-resistant and kept free from slippery substances or loose materials.

Arrangements should be made to minimise risks from ice and snow. This may involve gritting, snow clearing or even the closure of some routes particularly outside stairs, ladders and walkways on roofs.

### Further reading

HSE Watch your step: prevention of tripping, slipping and falling accidents at work.

## Falls or Falling Objects (Regulation 13)

The consequences of falling from heights or into dangerous substances are so serious that a high standard of protection is required. Secure fencing should normally be provided to prevent people falling from edges, and the fencing should also be adequate to prevent objects falling onto people. Where fencing cannot be provided, or has to be removed temporarily, other measures should be taken to prevent falls. Dangerous substances in tanks, pits or other structures should be securely fenced or covered.

Secure fencing should be provided wherever possible at any place where a person might fall 2 metres or more. Secure fencing should also be provided where a person might fall less than 2 metres where there are factors which increase the likelihood of a fall or the risk of serious injury; for example, where a traffic route passes close to an edge, or where a person might fall onto a dangerous surface or into the path of a vehicle. As a minimum, fencing should consist of two guard rails – a top rail and a lower rail – at a suitable height. The top of the fencing should be at least 1,100mm above the surface from which a person might fall. The fencing should be filled in sufficiently to prevent people or objects falling between the rails. The fencing should be of adequate strength and stability to restrain any person or object likely to fall against it, so chains, ropes or other non-rigid materials should not be used.

Staircases are the preferred method of providing access from one level to another. However, if a staircase is not practicable, a fixed ladder is permissible. In these Regulations a 'fixed ladder' includes a steep stairway on which safe ascent or descent requires a person to face the rungs or treads, and must meet the following specifications:

- Fixed ladders should be of sound construction, properly maintained and securely fixed. The rungs should be horizontal, give adequate foothold and not depend solely upon nails, screws or similar fixings for their support.
- Unless some other adequate handhold exists, the stiles of the ladder should extend 1,100mm above any landing served by the ladder or the highest rung used to step or stand on.
- Fixed ladders with a vertical height of more than 6 metres should normally have a landing or other adequate resting place every 6 metres. If possible, each 6-metre run should be out of line with the one below to reduce the distance a person might fall.
- Fixed ladders at an angle of less than 15° to the vertical which are more than 2.5 metres high should, where possible, be fitted with suitable safety hoops. The hoops should be no more than 900mm apart and start 2.5 metres from the base of the ladder. The top hoop should be in line with the top of the fencing on the platform served by the ladder.
- Where a ladder rises less than 2.5 metres, but is elevated so that a fall or more than 2 metres is possible, a single hoop should be placed in line with the top of the fencing.
- Where a ladder passes through a floor, the opening should be as small as possible.

Slips and trips which may be trivial at ground level can have more serious consequences when on a roof. It is therefore vital that precautions are taken, even when access is only occasional. Fragile roofs or surfaces should be clearly identified. A fragile roof is one which would be liable to fracture under a person's weight. All glazing, asbestos cement or similar sheeting should be treated as fragile unless there is firm evidence to the contrary. Care should be taken of old materials which may have become fragile because of corrosion. The risks may be increased by moss, lichen or ice etc.

Changes of level, such as a step between floors, which are not obvious should be marked to make them conspicuous.

Materials and objects should be stored and stacked in such a way that they are not likely to fall and cause injury. Racking should be of adequate strength and stability having regard to the loads placed on it and its vulnerability to damage, for example by vehicles.

The need for people to climb on top of vehicles or their loads should be avoided as far as possible. Where it is unavoidable, effective measures should be taken to prevent falls.

Scaffolding and other equipment used for temporary access may either follow the provisions of the Workplace Regulations (ACOP) or the requirements of the Construction Regulations.

*Further reading*

HSE: Effluent storage on farms, GS12.
HSE: Safety in roofwork, HS(G)33.
HSE: Stacking of bales in agriculture, IND(G)125L.
BS 6180:1982 Code of practice for protective barriers in and about buildings.
BS 5395:1985 Code of practice for the design of industrial type stairs, permanent ladders and walkways.
BS 6399:Part 3:1988 Design loading for buildings: code of practice for imposed roof loads.
HSE: Health & safety in retail and wholesale warehouses, HS(G)76.

## Transparent or Translucent Surfaces (Regulations 14, 15 & 16)

There are three Regulations specifically covering transparent and translucent surfaces. The first calls for transparent or translucent surfaces in doors, gates, walls and partitions to be of a safety material or to be adequately protected against breakage in the following cases:

- in doors and gates, and door and gate side panels where any part of the transparent or translucent surface is at shoulder level or below;
- in windows, walls and partitions where any part of the transparent or translucent surface is at waist level or below, except in glasshouses where people can be expected to be aware of glazing and to avoid contact.

The second Regulation states that it should be possible to reach and operate the control of openable windows, skylights and ventilators in a safe manner. Where necessary, window poles or similar equipment should be kept available, or a stable platform or other safe means of access should be provided. Controls should be so placed that people are not likely to fall through or out of the window. Where there is a danger of falling from a height, devices should be provided to prevent the window from opening too far. Open windows, skylights or ventilators should not project into an area where persons are likely to collide with them. The bottom edge of opening windows should normally be at least 800mm above floor level, unless there is a barrier to prevent falls.

Finally, the third Regulation states that all windows and skylights in a workplace must be of a design or be so constructed that they may be cleaned safely. Suitable provision should be made so that windows and skylights can be cleaned safely if they cannot be cleaned from the ground or other suitable surface.

*Further reading*

HSE: Prevention of falls to window cleaners, GS25.
HSE: Suspended access equipment, PM30.
BS 6206:1981 Specification for impact performance requirements for flat safety glass and safety plastics for use in buildings.
BS 6262:1982 Code of practice for glazing in buildings.
BS 8213:Part 1:1991 Windows, doors and rooflights: code of practice for safety in use and during cleaning of windows.

## Organization of Traffic Routes (Regulation 17)

The Regulation states that 'Every workplace must be organised in such a way that pedestrians and vehicles can circulate in a safe manner' and that 'Traffic routes in a workplace must be suitable for the persons or vehicles using them, sufficient in number and of sufficient size.'

Clear systems for routeing vehicles should be designed, preferably with vehicle routes segregated from pedestrian routes. Clear walkways should be protected by barriers painted with black and yellow stripes, and pedestrian crossings across vehicular routes should be clearly marked. Lorries should not be permitted to reverse in areas where pedestrians are likely to be unless marshalled by a trained person. Marshallers should be suitably dressed in high-visibility clothing, and ensure that drivers can see them and their signals at all times.

Loading bays should be provided with at least one exit point from the lower level. If this is not possible, a refuge should be available as shown in Figure 8.4 to enable persons to avoid being struck or crushed by a vehicle.

Potential hazards such as sharp bends, junctions and crossings must be indicated by suitable warning signs. Suitable road markings and signs should also be used to alert drivers to any restrictions which apply to the use of the route. Buildings, departments and entrances should be clearly marked to prevent unplanned manoeuvres. All signs used in connection with traffic control should comply with the Traffic Signs Regulations and General Directions 1981 and the Highway Code.

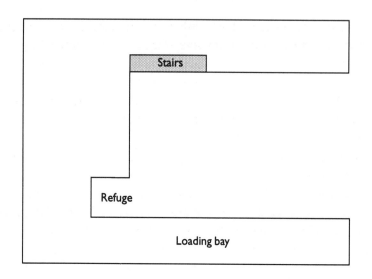

Figure 8.4: Provision of refuge area

*Further reading*

HSE: Road transport in factories and similar workplaces, GS 9 (Rev.).
HSE: Safety in working with lift trucks, HS(G)6 (Rev.).
HSE: Container terminals: Safe working practice, HS(G)7.
HSE: Danger! Transport at work, IND(G)22L.

## Doors and Gates (Regulation 18)

Doors and gates which swing in both directions should have a transparent panel except if they are low enough to see over. Conventionally hinged doors on main traffic routes should also be fitted with such panels. Panels should be positioned to enable a person in a wheelchair to be seen from the other side. Sliding doors should have a stop or other effective means to prevent the door coming off the end of the track. They should also have a retaining rail to prevent the door falling should the suspension system fail or the rollers leave the track. Upward opening doors should be fitted with an effective device such as a counter-balance or ratchet mechanism to prevent them falling back in a manner likely to cause injury. Power operated doors and gates should have safety features to prevent people being injured as a result of being struck or trapped. Safety features include:

- a sensitive edge, or other suitable detector, and associated trip device to stop, or reverse, the motion of the door or gate when obstructed;
- a device to limit the closing force so that it is insufficient to cause injury;
- an operating control which must be held in position during the whole of the closing motion. This will only be suitable where the risk of injury is low and the speed of closure is slow. Such a control, when released, should cause the door to stop or reopen immediately and should be positioned so that the operator has a clear view of the door throughout its movement.

Where necessary, power operated doors and gates should have a readily identifiable and accessible control switch or device so that they can be stopped quickly in an emergency. Normal on/off controls may be sufficient. It should be possible to open a power operated door or gate if the power supply fails, unless it opens automatically in such circumstances, or there is an alternative way through. This does not apply to lift doors and other doors and gates which are there to prevent falls or access to areas of potential danger. Where tools are necessary for manual opening they should be readily available at all times. If the power supply is restored while the door is being opened manually, the person opening it should not be put at risk.

### Sanitary and Washing Facilities (Regulations 20 & 21)

'Suitable and sufficient sanitary conveniences shall be provided at readily accessible places' and:

- the rooms containing them must be adequately ventilated and lit;
- they and the rooms containing them must be kept in a clean and orderly condition;
- separate rooms containing conveniences must be provided for men and women unless each convenience is in a separate room with a door lockable from the inside.

'Suitable and sufficient washing facilities, including showers if required by the nature of the work or for health reasons, shall be provided at readily accessible places' and:

- they must be provided in the immediate vicinity of every sanitary convenience, whether or not provided elsewhere as well;
- they must be provided in the vicinity of any changing rooms required by the Workplace Regulations, whether or not provided elsewhere as well;

- they must include a supply of clean hot and cold water (which must be running water so far as is practicable);
- they must include soap or other suitable means of cleaning;
- they must include towels or other suitable means of drying;
- the rooms containing them must be sufficiently ventilated and lit;
- they and the rooms containing them are kept in a clean and orderly condition;
- separate facilities must be provided for men and women unless they are provided for use by one person at a time and have a door which can be locked from the inside. (This sub-paragraph does not apply to facilities which are provided for washing hands, forearms and face only.)

For the purposes of this Regulation, the term 'facilities' means both sanitary and washing facilities.

Sufficient facilities should be provided to enable everyone at work to use them without undue delay. Minimum numbers of facilities are given in Figures 8.5 and 8.6 below, but more may be necessary if, for example, breaks are taken at set times or workers finish together and need to wash before leaving. Special provision should be made for any worker with a disability to have access to facilities which are suitable for his use.

| Number of people at work | Number of WCs | Number of washstations |
| --- | --- | --- |
| 1–5 | 1 | 1 |
| 6–25 | 2 | 2 |
| 26–50 | 3 | 3 |
| 51–75 | 4 | 4 |
| 76–100 | 5 | 5 |

Figure 8.5

The number of people at work shown in column 1 above refers to the maximum number likely to be in the workplace at any one time. Where separate sanitary accommodation is provided for a group of workers, for example men, women, office workers or manual workers, a separate calculation should be made for each group.

| Number of men at work | Number of WCs | Number of urinals |
|---|---|---|
| 1–15 | 1 | 1 |
| 16–30 | 2 | 1 |
| 31–45 | 2 | 2 |
| 45–60 | 3 | 2 |
| 61–75 | 3 | 3 |
| 76–90 | 4 | 3 |
| 91–100 | 4 | 4 |

Figure 8.6

Figure 8.6 may be used for calculating facilities used only by men. A urinal may be either an individual urinal or a section of urinal space which is at least 600mm long.

An additional WC and one additional washing station should be provided for every 25 people above 100 (or fraction of 25). In the case of WCs used by men only, an additional WC for every 50 men (or fraction of 50) above 100 is sufficient provided at least an equal number of additional urinals are provided.

## Drinking Water (Regulation 22)

An adequate supply of wholesome drinking water must be provided for all persons at work in the workplace. Drinking water should normally be obtained from a public or private water supply by means of a tap on a pipe connected directly to the water main. Water should only be provided in refillable containers where it cannot be obtained from a main supply. Such containers should be suitably enclosed to prevent contamination, and should be refilled at least daily.

Drinking cups or beakers should be provided unless the supply is by means of a drinking fountain. If any chance exists of any person drinking from a water supply that is not meant for drinking, the drinking water supplies must be clearly marked.

## Accommodation for Clothing (Regulation 23)

Accommodation should be provided for work clothing and workers' own personal clothing to be hung in a clean, warm, dry, well-ventilated place where it can dry out during the course of a working day, if necessary. If the workroom is unsuitable for this purpose, accommodation should be provided in another convenient place. The accommodation should consist of at least a separate hook or peg for each worker.

Where work clothing which is not taken home becomes dirty, damp or contaminated due to the work, it should be accommodated separately from the worker's own clothing. Where work clothing becomes wet, the facilities should enable it to be dried out by the beginning of the following work period unless other dry clothing is provided.

*Further reading*
Personal Protective Equipment at Work Regulations 1992.
HSE: Guidance on Personal Protective Equipment at Work Regulations 1992, L25.

## Facilities for Changing Clothing (Regulation 24)

Suitable and sufficient facilities must be provided for any person at work in the workplace to change clothing in all cases where:

- the person has to wear special clothing for work;
- the person cannot, for reasons of health or propriety, be expected to change in another room.

Changing facilities should be readily accessible from workrooms and eating facilities. They should be provided with adequate seating, and should contain clothing accommodation and washing facilities. The facilities should be constructed and arranged to ensure the privacy of the user.

## Facilities for Rest and to Eat Meals (Regulation 25)

Suitable and sufficient rest facilities must be provided at readily accessible places.

Seats should be provided for workers to use during breaks, and should be in a place where personal protective equipment need not be worn. In offices and other reasonably clean workplaces, work seats or other seats in the work area will suffice provided workers are not subject to excessive disturbance during breaks. Eating facilities should include a facility for preparing or obtaining a hot drink, such as an electric kettle, a vending machine or a canteen. Such facilities should be kept to a clean hygienic standard, and the responsibility for cleaning clearly allocated.

Facilities for pregnant women and nursing mothers to rest should be conveniently situated in relation to sanitary facilities and, where necessary, include the facility to lie down.

Rest areas and rest rooms should be arranged to enable employees to use them without experiencing discomfort from tobacco smoke. This can be achieved by the provision of separate areas or rooms for smokers or non-smokers, or by prohibiting smoking in rest areas and rest rooms.

*Further reading*
HSE: Occupational health aspects of pregnancy, MA 6.
HSE: Passive smoking at work, IND(G)63L.

# CHAPTER 9

# Fire

## The Legislation

The general requirements for fire safety are laid down in the Fire Precautions Act of 1971 (FPA), which is the basic standard that every fire authority works to. The FPA applies to all premises except private single dwellings. Where a fire certificate is in force under the Act, it will set specific requirements for the particular premises to which it relates.

The Fire Precautions (Places of Work) Regulations 1995 (FPR95) were issued to reinforce the FPA and to close loopholes in the Act. FPR95 covers the following:

- all employers' premises;
- all premises to which the public have access;
- all self-employed persons who have one or more employees;
- hotels and boarding houses with more than six beds;
- Crown-occupied buildings, e.g. prisons;
- voluntary organizations with one or more employees.

FPR95 lay down minimum legal standards for fire precautions and fire safety as follows:

- **Fire Doors.** All internal and external fire doors must be made of solid fire and smoke-resisting material. They must give at least 30 minutes protection in low- or medium-risk workplaces, and 60 minutes protection in high risk premises.
- **Direction.** All fire doors, doors opening on to staircases or corridors and other doors affording exit from workplaces where more than 50 people work must open outwards.
- **Exit signs and lighting.** Every door, window or other exit (other than the main exit), access room and egress route affording means of escape must have 'FIRE EXIT' notices affixed to them. Artificial lighting must be provided from a mains or back-up generator supply during the hours of

darkness or in areas that do not otherwise have natural or artificial light. Emergency lighting must be provided in case the artificial lighting powered from the mains fails.

- **Lifts and hoists.** Every lift or hoist must be completely enclosed with fire-resisting material and doors that afford 30 minutes protection.
- **Locks.** Doors must not be locked or fastened so as to deny immediate use during working hours.
- **Keys.** A key in the lock or a glass case or a glass release bolt are no longer permitted. Where such exist, they must be removed and a suitable mechanism fitted, such as a push-bar quick-release mechanism.
- **Fire alarms.** Fire alarms must be indicated, and records maintained of types, numbers, locations and servicing of all alarm systems.
- **Equipment.** Fire-fighting equipment appropriate to the situation must be provided, taking into account:
  – the size, design, construction and content of the workplace;
  – the nature of the activity in the workplace;
  – the fire risk assessment.
  The equipment must be readily accessible, maintained in good working order, clearly indicated and regularly serviced. Signs made to BS5499 must be displayed to indicate the location and correct siting of such equipment. Portable equipment must be immediately available for use, access to it must not be blocked and it must be serviceable for use.
- **Clearways.** All fire doors, access routes to them and egress routes away from them or from the building must be kept clear at all times. This includes the arrangements of the contents of working rooms, which must be laid out in such a way that MOE can be reached easily without obstruction.
- **Automatic systems.** There must be an automatic fire detection system fitted where the outbreak of fire is unlikely to be noticed before a life-threatening situation arises.

## Means of Escape

The main principle of fire safety is that people must be able to proceed safely along a recognizable escape route, by their own unaided efforts, to a place of safety regardless of the location of the fire. It is, therefore, means of exit to a place of safety that is of concern, but the v the place of work to that exit. The following factors shoul when defining a Means of Escape (MOE):

- the results of the risk assessment;
- occupant capacity v. exit capacity;
- the distance of travel required from the workplace to a place of safety;
- alternative means of escape;
- the signs directing people to the exits, and the exit signs on doors;
- the lighting in escape routes – both normal and emergency;
- the location of a place of safety away from the building;
- the width of the MOE – it must not be less than 1.05 metres;
- the number of exits from each workroom or storey.

The following should not be included in a MOE:

- lifts (except those designated for safe evacuation of the disabled);
- escalators;
- self-rescue and lowering devices.

MOE must not be used as a temporary store for furniture; nor should portable heaters or any other equipment be placed within them. It is illegal not to keep a designated MOE clear.

## Fire Certificates

An employer or keeper of premises must apply to the local fire authority for a fire certificate for:

- any place of work where more than 20 people are at work on the ground or lower floors;
- any place of work where more than 10 people are at work above ground level;
- a building where highly flammable or explosive substances are stored or used in or under the premises;
- sleeping accommodation in a hotel or boarding house that:
  – accommodates more than six people;
  – is above the first floor;
  – is below ground level;
- places of entertainment;
- licensed premises.

The term 'at work' means not just those who are actually employed, but all ge who are working in the premises. Visitors, contractors and customers need not be counted in the total of persons 'at work'. Persons on training for employment are normally counted towards the total, but this may vary. The local fire authority should be contacted for a ruling on this point.

A fire certificate will specify:

- the particular use or uses of the premises it covers;
- the means of escape the premises are to have;
- the means for ensuring that the MOE can be safely and effectively used at all times when the building is in use;
- the measures to prevent the spread of fire, smoke and fumes;
- the emergency lighting and direction signs required;
- the means to be provided for first-aid fire fighting by persons in the building;
- the means for giving warning in the event of fire;
- for factories, details of explosive or highly flammable substances stored or used on the premises;
- maintenance of the MOE keeping them free from obstruction;
- maintenance of other fire precautions specified in the certificate;
- the training to be given to persons employed on the premises;
- the maximum number of persons permitted to be on the premises, on each floor, at any one time;
- any other fire precautions relevant to the building and its use.

## Fire Risk Assessment

The basic rules for risk assessments are given in Chapter 7, and apply equally to fire risk assessments. A suggested six-stage fire risk assessment is shown in Figure 9.1. Written fire risk assessments are required for all employers who have five or more employees; these assessments should be submitted to the local fire authority. Before the risk assessment can be carried out, it is first necessary to determine the risk classification of the premises.

All premises fall into one of three levels of risk classification:

- **Low risk.** This is the lowest category – there is no such thing as 'no-risk' premises. The classification 'low-risk' means that the risk of fire occurring or, if it does occur, the risk of flames, smoke or gases spreading is negligible. Examples might be workplaces used for heavy engineering, or processes that are entirely wet and/or use only non-combustible materials. Offices and shops are most unlikely to be classified as 'low-risk', while premises with sleeping accommodation will never be 'low-risk'.

**Stage1: Identify hazards**

What can burn? What quantities are there? What are the ignition sources? Common sense needs to be applied here. There is little point in noting every electrical switch or light-fitting, but blanket phrases such as 'normal combustibles' or 'normal ignition sources' are probably too bland. What is needed is a general description plus specific noting of out-of-the-ordinary hazards.

**Stage 2: Identify those at risk**

Who can be affected by fire? What numbers are involved? Are they employees or could members of the public also be involved? Are they disabled?

**Stage 3: Consider fire precautions**

This is the heart of the task. Basically all aspects of fire precautions need to be assessed against good practice. Consider:

- basic housekeeping standards;
- control of flammable liquids and gases;
- emergency lighting;
- fire brigade access;
- fire compartmentation and other passive measures;
- fire detection and alarm;
- first-aid fire fighting equipment;
- fixed fire fighting equipment;
- maintenance of electrical equipment;
- means of escape (MOE);
- signage;
- smoke control;
- staff training;
- written procedures and documentation.

In fact, everything! Are the fire precautions adequate and appropriate to the risk?

**Stage 4: Consider improvements, make recommendations**

If precautions are considered to be inadequate, then recommendations for improvements to bring them up to an adequate level need to be made. (Alternatively a more detailed, but not necessarily quantified, risk assessment may be needed to better assess the risk.) The spirit of risk assessment, however, is that risks should be reduced to as low as reasonably practicable. So consideration should also be given to any low-cost improvements that can be implemented easily even if overall the risk is not considered to be excessive. A classic example would be the substitution of a flammable solvent by a water-based one.

**Stage 5: Record, prepare emergency plan**

The assessment should be recorded. In addition, fire emergency plans (in the smallest premises this is just a Fire Action Notice) should be produced.

**Stage 6: Review**

The assessment should be reviewed whenever there are material changes to the circumstances.

Figure 9.1: Six-stage fire risk assessment

- **Normal risk.** Premises of 'normal risk' are ones where:
  - any outbreak of fire is likely to remain localized;
  - fire is likely to spread slowly;
  - the risk of any part of the structure burning is small;
  - the risk of burning materials producing large quantities of life-threatening smoke or gas is minimal.

  Such 'normal-risk' premises and the hazards in them would include workplaces with brick walls, timber floors and roof trusses, and no undesirable features. Premises may include shops, offices and other places where large numbers of people are unlikely to be present.
- **High risk.** It follows that everything else is classified as 'high risk'. Factors that may place premises in the 'high-risk' category include:
  - premises used for sleeping accommodation;
  - young children or the elderly are present;
  - highly flammable substances are present;
  - airborne dust is present;
  - inadequate fire-resisting partitioning;
  - vertical or horizontal openings, gaps, cracks or holes through which flames, smoke or gases could pass;
  - long and/or complicated MOE;
  - flammable or smoke-producing finishes on walls, ceilings or floors;
  - naked flames are in use;
  - excessive heat is generated;
  - large kitchens serving restaurants or canteens etc.;
  - central fuel storage facilities;
  - the presence of upholstered furniture which may give off toxic fumes or smoke when burning;
  - waste storage and disposal areas.

The list is not exhaustive. If in doubt contact the local fire authority.

# CHAPTER 10

# Plant and Machinery

## Legislation

Many serious accidents at work involve machinery. Hair or clothing can become entangled in rotating parts; shearing can occur between two parts moving past one another; and people can be struck by moving parts. Twelve per cent of all deaths and reportable injuries suffered in industry are caused while operating machinery.

The Provision and Use of Work Equipment Regulations 1992 became effective on 1 January 1993 and were implemented in stages until 1 January 1997. They are summarized below:

- in selecting work equipment, the working conditions and hazards in the workplace must be taken into account;
- additional hazards that may be created by installation and use of work equipment must also be taken into account;
- all work equipment must be suitable for the purpose for which it is intended;
- all work equipment must be properly maintained and must be designed to facilitate safe maintenance operations;
- where specific risks exist in relation to the use of work equipment, the use of that equipment must be restricted to those who have been appointed and properly trained to use it;
- adequate information, instruction and training must be given to all employees in the use of work equipment.

The scope of 'work equipment' is extremely wide. It includes:

- single machines such as a power press, guillotine, circular saw bench, photocopier or a combine harvester;
- tools such as a portable drill or a hammer;
- apparatus such as a Bunsen burner or other laboratory equipment;

- any assembly arranged and controlled to function as a whole such as a bottling plant or a robot line;
- motor vehicles which are not privately owned (however, when used on the public highway more specific road traffic legislation will take precedence).

## Machinery Safety

The principal duty under the Regulations is to take effective measures to prevent contact with dangerous parts of machinery. The measures must either prevent access to the dangerous part, or stop the movement of the dangerous part before any part of a person can reach it. The Regulation lays down a hierarchy of preventative measures:

- fit fixed guards or other protective devices to prevent access to any dangerous part of machinery or to any rotating stock bar;
- fit fail-safe devices to stop the movement of dangerous parts of machinery when guards are removed;
- provide jigs, holders or push-sticks;
- provide information, instruction and training to all users in the safe operation of all the work equipment they use, and to provide effective supervision.

Some prescribed dangerous machines can only be used by 'young persons' (under 18 but over school-leaving age) after full instruction and sufficient training and under full supervision. Examples include guillotines, mixers, bacon and vegetable slicers and power operated wrappers. Children must never be allowed to operate or help at machines. All machine operators must be trained and given any necessary protective clothing. Adequate lighting must be provided for all machines.

A suggested Equipment Record showing specific hazards and personnel trained to operate the equipment is at Figure 10.1.

## Machine controls

The Regulations require the provision of controls and certain arrangements where appropriate. A control is the manual actuator that the operator touches, e.g. a button, foot-pedal, knob or lever. It may operate directly, but is more often a part of a control device such as a brake, clutch, switch or relay. The control and

**Equipment:**

Location:

---

**Maintenance contract**

Company:                    Number:                    Renewal date:

---

**Specific hazards:**

---

**Personnel trained to operate this equipment:**

Name:                                                        Date:

Figure 10.1: Equipment record

control devices are parts of the control system which may be considered as all the components which act together to monitor and control the functions of the work equipment. Control systems may operate using mechanical linkages, electricity, pneumatics, hydraulics or a combination of these.

Employers must:

- ensure that control switches are clearly marked to show what they do;
- have emergency stop controls if necessary such as mushroom-head push buttons within easy reach;
- make sure that operating controls are designed and placed to prevent accidental operation, e.g. by shrouding start buttons and pedals.

## Machinery Maintenance

It is important that equipment is maintained so that its performance does not deteriorate to the extent that it puts people at risk. The extent and complexity of maintenance varies enormously, from identifying a loose head on a hammer to a substantial integrated programme for a complex processing plant. Equipment may need to be checked frequently to ensure that safety-related features are functioning correctly. A fault which affects production is normally apparent within a short time, but a fault in a safety-critical system could remain undetected unless maintenance procedures provide adequate inspection and testing. The frequency at which equipment needs to be checked is dependent on the equipment itself and the risk involved; it could be annually, every three months, or even daily.

The Regulations do not call for a maintenance log but it is recommended that a record of maintenance be kept. If there is a log it must be kept up-to-date to provide information for future planning, and to inform maintenance personnel of previous action taken.

## Stability of Work Equipment

There are many types of work equipment that might fall over, collapse or overturn unless suitable precautions are taken to fix them to the ground, stabilize them, or tie, fasten or clamp them in some way.

### Fixed work equipment

Most machines used in a fixed position should be bolted or otherwise fastened down so that they do not move or rock during use. Machinery can move imperceptibly during operation especially where there are vibrations; clamping or bolting will prevent movement or rocking.

### Mobile work equipment

Certain types of mobile equipment, for example mobile cranes or access platforms, while inherently stable when not lifting, can have their stability increased during use by means of outriggers or similar devices. Every item of equipment has its limits and should not be used beyond the stated load or over unsuitable terrain.

## Pressurized Plant and Systems

The Pressure Systems and Transportable Gas Containers Regulations 1989 (PSTGC Regs) provide a comprehensive framework covering all types of pressure vessels and pressurized systems from compressed air in a garage to the largest chemical plant, and all types of transportable gas containers.

The Regulations state that:

- all plant and systems must be designed, constructed and installed to prevent danger and must have safety devices;
- systems must be properly maintained;
- any modifications or repairs must not give rise to danger;
- there must be a written scheme for examination of pressure vessels, fittings and pipework drawn up by a competent person;
- the examinations must be carried out;
- records must be kept;
- the plant must be operated within safe operating limits. Sometimes these are laid down by the manufacturer or supplier. If not, a competent person should be called in to assist;
- employers must provide adequate instructions – this should include the manufacturer's operating manual;
- instructions must be provided on what to do in an emergency.

Before commencing a job, it is worth asking whether it can be done another way without using pressurized equipment. If possible, low pressure or vacuum should be used in preference to high pressure.

Remember! Horseplay with compressed air is dangerous.

*Further reading*
HSE: A guide to the PSTGC Regulations 1989, HS(R)30.
HSE: Compressed air safety, HS(G)39 (Rev.).


## Handling and Transportation

Common hazards are the manual movement of loads and frequent forced or awkward movements of the body leading, for example, to back injuries or severe pain in the hand, wrist, arm or neck. Moving materials mechanically is also hazardous and people can be crushed or struck by material when it falls from a lifting or moving device, or is dislodged from a storage stack.

Every year, over 5,000 accidents involving transport in the workplace are reported. Over 60 of these accidents result in death. People are knocked over, run over or crushed against fixed objects by powered vehicles, plant and trailers which roll away when incorrectly parked. This section deals with what is moved, how and where.

### Manual handling

Manual handling must be avoided if a safer way is practicable. Jobs should be designed to fit the work to the person rather than the person to the work. Employers and employees must:

- avoid manual handling where there is a risk of injury;
- assess the risk of injury from any hazardous manual handling that cannot be avoided;
- reduce the risk of injury from hazardous manual handling.

Consider the possibility of providing mechanical help such as a sack truck or hoist. Can the loads be made smaller or lighter or easier to grasp? Change the system of work to reduce the effort required. Improve the layout of the workplace to make the work more efficient. Personal protective equipment for the hands and feet may reduce the risk.

The Manual Handling Operations Regulations 1992 give detailed advice on mechanical handling.

### Lifting by machine

Safe lifting by machine needs to be planned. Any equipment used must have been properly designed, manufactured and tested. In planning the lift, consider what is being lifted: its weight; its centre of gravity; how to attach it to the lifting machinery; who is in control of the lift; and the safe limits of the equipment. Rehearse the lift if necessary.

- Use only certified lifting equipment, marked with its safe working load (SWL), which is not overdue for examination.
- Keep the test certificate for all lifting machinery and tackle showing its SWL and the annual or six-monthly examination reports.
- Never use unsuitable equipment such as makeshift, damaged or badly worn chains, kinked or twisted wire ropes, or frayed or rotted fibre ropes.
- Never exceed the SWL of the machine or tackle.
- Do not lift a load if its weight or the adequacy of the equipment is in doubt.
- Make sure that the load is properly attached to the lifting equipment. If necessary, securely bind the load to prevent it slipping or falling off.
- Before lifting an unbalanced load find its centre of gravity by raising it just a few inches off the ground – there is less likelihood of harm if it should drop.
- Use packing to prevent any sharp edges on the load damaging slings. Do not allow tackle to be damaged by being dropped or dragged from under loads.
- When using jib cranes ensure that the load radius indicator and/or automatic safe load indicator is correctly set.
- Outriggers must be used where necessary.
- When using multi-slings take the sling angle into account.
- Have a responsible slinger or banksman using a recognized signalling system.

*Further reading*
HSE: Safety in working with lift-trucks.
HSE: Lighten the load: guidance for employers on musculoskeletal disorders, IND(G)109(L).
HSE: Getting to grips with manual handling: a short guide for employers, IND(G)143(L).
Manual Handling Operations Regulations 1992.
HSE: Reversing vehicles, IND(G)148(L).

## Noise

Loud noise at work can cause irreversible hearing damage. It accelerates the normal hearing loss which occurs as we grow older. It can cause other problems such as tinnitus, interference with communications or stress. Noise is measured in decibels – usually written as dB(A). The noise level – loudness – is measured on a scale from silent (0 dB(A)) to 140 dB(A) in the noisiest situations. In most jobs, the risk depends not just on the noise levels but for how long people are exposed to them. The total amount of noise exposure over the whole working day is called the 'daily personal noise exposure' – usually shortened to $L_{EP,d}$. If needed, noise levels should be checked by a competent person who understands and can apply the HSE's guidance on noise measurement.

The purpose of the Noise at Work Regulations 1989 is to reduce hearing damage caused by loud noise; they lay down three action levels. Employers are required to take action when noise reaches the 85 dB(A) 'first action' level. Further action is required if the noise reaches the 90 dB(A) 'second action' or the 140 dB(A) 'peak action' levels. As a guide, if normal speech cannot be heard clearly from a distance of 2 metres, the level is likely to be around 85 dB(A). If the same applies from a distance of 1 metre, the level is likely to be around 90 dB(A).

Figure 10.2 shows some typical noise levels.

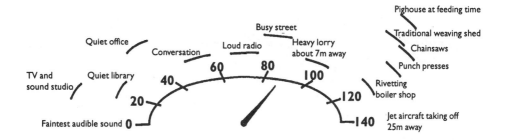

Figure 10.2: Range of typical noise levels

At the first action level the employer must:

- have the risk assessed by a competent person;
- tell the workers about the risks and precautions;
- make hearing protection freely available to those who want it where the levels exceed 85 dB(A);
- suggest that workers take medical advice if they think their hearing is being affected.

At the second level the employer must:

- do all that is possible to reduce exposure to the noise other than by providing hearing protection, e.g. engineering control;
- mark zones where noise reaches the second action level with recognized signs to restrict entry. People must not enter these zones unless wearing hearing protection.

*Further reading*
HSE: Introducing the Noise at Work Regulations, IND(G)75(L).
HSE: Noise at work: advice for employees, IND(G)99(L).
HSE: Noise in construction, IND(G)127(L).

## Vibration

Vibration is often associated with noise, but it is difficult to measure. Excessive exposure through the use of hand-held power tools and machinery such as chipping hammers, grinders and chainsaws can cause hand-arm vibration syndrome (HAVS) – a painful condition affecting blood circulation, nerves, muscles and bones in the hands and arms. Its best-known effect is vibration white finger (VWF). Whole body vibration (WBV) mainly affects drivers of vehicles such as dumpers, tractors and lift trucks and can cause low back pain and spinal damage.

Unlike noise, there are no particular Regulations specific to vibration. However, where a hazard exists, the Management of Health and Safety at Work Regulations 1992 and the Provision and Use of Work Equipment Regulations 1992 apply.

To reduce the effects of vibration consider:

- providing work breaks or work sharing to reduce exposure time;
- keeping the hands and body warm by wearing gloves, for instance. It should be noted, however, that there are no gloves which provide effective protection against vibration;
- advising people to exercise their fingers to improve the blood flow.

## Radiations

Visible light is just one part of the spectrum of electro-magnetic radiation. It ranges from radio waves at one end to ultraviolet light and gamma rays at the other. Exposure to all kinds of radiation should be reduced wherever possible. Where the hazard arises from the process or the equipment used, it may be possible to use something safer. Checks on the radiation hazard should be made at the time of purchase. Figure 10.3 shows where various types of radiation are likely to be found, and identifies some of the effects they can cause.

| Hazard | Emitted from | Possible effects |
|---|---|---|
| Radio frequency and microwaves | Plastics welding; some communications; catering; drying and heating equipment | Excessive heating of any exposed parts of the body |
| Infra-red | Any glowing source, e.g. glass production, and some lasers | Reddening of the skin, burns and cataracts |
| Visible radiation | All high-intensity visible light sources; high-intensity beams such as from some lasers can be especially damaging | Heating and destruction of tissue of the eyes or skin |
| Ultraviolet (UV) | Welding; some lasers; mercury vapour lamps; carbon arcs; the sun | Sunburn, conjunctivitis, arc eye, skin cancer, production of toxic levels of ozone |
| Ionizing radiations (X-rays, gamma rays and particulate radiation) | Radiation generators; some high-voltage equipment; radiography equipment and containers; other radioactive substances including radon gas | Burns, dermatitis, cancer, cell damage or blood changes, cataracts |

Figure 10.3

*Further reading*
Ionising Radiation Regulations 1985, IRR85.
Ionising Radiations (Outside Workers) Regulations 1993.
ACOP: Dose limitation: restriction of exposure.
HSE: Keep your top on, IND(G)147(L).

## Electricity

The three main hazards are contact with live parts, fire and explosion. Each year roughly 1,000 accidents at work involving shock or burn are reported and about 30 of these are fatal. Fires started by poor electrical installations cause many other deaths and injuries. Explosions are caused by electrical apparatus or static electricity igniting flammable vapours or dusts.

Employers are required to carry out assessments of all electrical installations, apparatus and equipment, even down to inspecting fuses in electric plugs. The full requirements are contained in the Electricity at Work Regulations 1989. Many of the tasks carried out routinely and without thought of danger fall within the scope of the Regulations. For example:

- changing light bulbs or fluorescent tubes and their starter units;
- changing fuses;
- plugging in and out of sockets;
- creating new circuitry by using extension leads;
- switching on and off at switches and mains isolators;
- withdrawing fuses when minor electrical work is carried out;
- moving the position of portable electrical equipment;
- fitting 13 amp plugs;
- purchase and use of portable electric devices.

While the changing of a light bulb is a basic task, the fact remains that management have to satisfy themselves the person carrying out such tasks are 'competent'.

All portable appliances and 'pluggable' equipment should be inspected by a competent electrician at an agreed frequency, and records of such inspections kept in an electricity log. The frequency of inspections will depend upon the use to which the equipment is put. For instance, portable equipment such as videos or overhead projectors may need to be inspected more often than a computer that remains in one office for the whole of its working life. The assessor carrying out the inspection should ensure that all inspected items carry a unique code of endorsement that gives the certification date. All employees should be instructed not to use equipment that is not 'in-date', and to report any such equipment to their manager or safety officer.

Managers should not allow any private or personal item of electrical equipment to be used in the workplace. Such equipment is often discarded at home and brought to work to be used for a little longer. These items are usually old when brought onto the premises, get the worst kind of treatment and are most prone to causing accidents.

*Further reading*

HSE: Electricity at work: safe working practices, HS(G)85.

HSE: Maintenance of portable and transportable electrical equipment, HS(G)107.

HSE: Safe use of portable electrical equipment, PM(32) Rev.

HSE: Memorandum of guidance on the Electricity at Work Regulations 1989.

# CHAPTER 11

# Substances

Many substances can hurt and cause damage if they get into the body. Exposure can have an immediate effect, and repeated exposure can damage the liver, lungs or other organs. Some substances may cause asthma and many can damage the skin. Special care is needed when handling cancer-causing substances (carcinogens).

## COSHH

The Control of Substances Hazardous to Health Regulations 1988 (COSHH) gives the full legal requirement for all hazardous substances. Section 2 of the COSHH Regulations defines a hazardous substance as one which falls into any of the following five categories:

- that substance which is classified as toxic, very toxic, irritant, harmful, corrosive, flammable, explosive or radioactive under the Chemicals (Hazard Information and Packaging) Regulations 1993 (CHIP);
- any substance for which a MEL has been set in Schedule 1 of COSHH or which has an OES set by HSC. [MEL stands for 'Maximum Exposure Limit' which means the maximum airborne concentration of any substance up to which an employee is permitted to be exposed during a reference period – usually expressed as a time-weighted average (TWA) of minutes or hours, e.g. 15-minute TWA or 12-hour TWA. OES, the 'Occupational Exposure Standard', is the maximum airborne concentration of certain substances down to which emissions into the working environment must be controlled. HSE Guidance Note EH40 lists MELs and OESs, and is updated annually];
- any micro-organism that creates a hazard to the health of any person, such as legionellae which causes Legionnaires' Disease;
- any dust particles in a substantial airborne concentration;
- any other substance not mentioned above that creates a comparable risk of ill-health effects to any person.

The COSHH Regulations cover any hazardous substance that is included in the five categories above, and includes any natural or artificial substance that is solid, liquid, dust, gas or vapour. The following substances are subject to their own COSHH-style regulations:

- lead;
- asbestos;
- explosive or flammable substances;
- mining substances used below ground;
- substances used in medical treatments.

NO employer, no matter how small the workforce, or whatever their industry, is exempt from COSHH – not even the self-employed. Even if the result of carrying out the procedures is a nil-return, they must be followed.

*COSHH assessment*

A COSHH assessment must be carried out, and should include the following steps:

- Identify and list each substance giving:
  - name and chemical formula (if applicable);
  - how it is recognized (colour, smell, consistency etc.);
  - manufacturer or supplier;
  - its classification ('toxic' etc. as given under the first hazardous category above. This is usually shown on the label or the product data sheet. If not shown on either, contact the supplier);
  - its MEL;
  - its OES;
  - any other identification (micro-organism, dust etc.).
- Determine the hazard:
  - is it poisonous, carcinogenic or noxious;
  - are there any ill-health effects if it is inhaled, ingested or touches the skin (systemic).
- Assess the risk:
  - what is the degree of risk to which persons are exposed;
  - is the substance open to direct contact or is it enclosed;
  - how likely is it that a person may come into contact with it and be adversely affected by it.
- Determine the medical treatment needed:
  - even substances which are normally enclosed can be released by

spillage, leakage or explosion. What first-aid treatment would be required to cope with this?

A suggested layout for the COSHH assessment is given in Appendix C together with an example of a completed assessment showing that even substances widely used, both commercially and domestically, can be a hazard. Appendix C also contains a COSHH assessment checklist to assist in the identification of risks and the precautions taken.

### Control the risk

Having made the assessment of hazardous substances used in the workplace, the next step is to take the necessary measures to prevent or control the risk. Ideally, the hazard should be removed by using a safer material or changing the process. The COSHH Regulations state that 'every employer shall ensure that the exposure of his employees to substances hazardous to health is either prevented or, where this is not reasonably practicable, adequately controlled'. If the hazard cannot be removed, the following should be considered:

- Isolate or enclose:
  - put the harmful substance or process in a separate room or building or outside (but secure from the public);
  - reduce the amount used and the number of people exposed, and the time they are exposed for;
  - use closed transfer and handling systems.
- Local exhaust ventilation:
  - use a local exhaust ventilation (LEV) system which sucks dust or vapour through a small hood or booth, and takes it away from the worker.
- General ventilation:
  - a good supply and circulation of fresh air will help to dilute minor contamination.
- Good housekeeping:
  - do not store chemicals in open containers such as bottles or jam-jars – make sure the labels are not damaged, obscured or covered up;
  - keep dangerous chemicals locked away;
  - clear up spillages quickly and safely;
  - have smooth work surfaces to ensure easy cleaning;
  - clean regularly using a 'dust-free' method such as a vacuum system with a high efficiency filter;
  - keep dusty materials, waste and dirty rags in covered containers.

- Good welfare and personal hygiene:
  - do not smoke, eat or drink in chemical handling areas;
  - do not siphon or pipette hazardous chemicals by mouth – use a pump or hand-operated siphon;
  - do not transfer contamination, e.g. by putting pens or pencils in the mouth;
  - do remove protective clothing and wash hands before smoking, eating or drinking.
- Personal protective equipment (PPE):
  - PPE should only be used as a last resort if the exposure cannot be controlled as outlined above.

*Further reading*

HSE: Occupational exposure limits (updated annually), EH40.
HSE: Dust: general principles of protection, EH44.
HSE: Introduction to local exhaust ventilation, HS(G)37.
HSE: Step by step guide to COSHH assessment, HS(G)97.
HSE: COSHH: a brief guide for employers, IND(G)136(L).
HSE: An introduction to the Employment Medical Advisory Service, HSE5(Rev.).

## Lead

Work which exposes people to lead or its compounds is covered by the Control of Lead at Work Regulations 1980 and an ACOP. Risks may arise when lead dust or fumes are breathed in; powder, dust, paint or paste swallowed; or compounds taken in through the skin. As well as obvious work such as high temperature melting, making batteries or repairing radiators, there may be risk from repair or demolition of structures which have been painted with lead-based paints.

*Further reading*

Control of Lead at Work Regulations 1980.
HSE: Control of lead at work, COP2.

## Asbestos

Asbestos has been widely used, for example, as lagging on plant and pipework, in insulation products such as fireproofing panels, in asbestos cement roofing materials, and as sprayed coatings on structural steelworks to insulate against fire and noise. All types of asbestos can be dangerous if disturbed. The danger arises when asbestos fibres as a very fine dust become airborne and are breathed in. Exposure can cause diseases such as lung cancer. Well-sealed, undamaged asbestos is often best left alone. Make sure that all asbestos is sealed and protected against damage. If it cannot be sealed and protected and is likely to give off dust, it may need to be removed. All work on asbestos and the precautions needed, including respirators, are covered by the Control of Asbestos at Work Regulations 1987.

*Further reading*
Control of Asbestos at Work Regulations 1987.
HSE: Asbestos – exposure limits, EH10(Rev.).
HSE: Work with asbestos insulating board, EH37(Rev.).

## Flammable and Explosive Substances

Some gases, liquids and solids can cause fire or explosions. For a fire to start, fuel, air and a source of ignition are needed. Common materials may burn violently at high temperatures in oxygen-rich conditions, e.g. when a gas cylinder is leaking. Some dusts form a cloud which will explode when ignited. A small explosion can disturb dust and create a second explosion severe enough to destroy a building.

There is little general law. Flammable liquids and LPG are covered by the Highly Flammable Liquids and Liquefied Petroleum Gases Regulations 1972. Even if a small quantity of petrol or petroleum mixture is stored, a licence may be needed under the Petroleum Acts – check with the local authority. Suppliers should consult the Chemicals (Hazard Information and Packaging) Regulations 1993.

*Further reading*
HSE: CHIP for everyone, HS(G)108.
HSE: The complete idiot's guide to CHIP, IND(G)151(L).
HSE: Storage of flammable liquids, HS(G)50 to 52.
HSE: Assessment of fire hazards, HS(G)64.
HSE: Solvents and you, IND(G)93(L) (Rev.).
HSE: A guide to the Control of Explosives Regulations 1991, L10.

# CHAPTER 12

# Procedures

Chapters 8 to 11 have looked at particular hazards. This chapter deals more generally with safe procedures and the systems of work needed to deal with them. Section 2 of HASWA requires 'safe systems of work', but does not go into detail. The following information is taken from the HSE publication 'Essentials of Health and Safety at Work':

## Clear Procedures

Having clear procedures helps to get things right and to check that work is being done safely. For serious hazards and risks it is worth writing them down, e.g. a written 'permit to work'. This will not be necessary for many ordinary jobs.

When looking at systems, don't forget:

- routine work (including setting up and preparation, finishing off and cleaning activities);
- less routine work (e.g. maintenance);
- emergencies (e.g. fire, spillages or plant breakdown).

## Safe Procedures

Think about:

- Who is in charge of the job?
- Do the responsibilities overlap with anyone else's?
- Is there anything which is not someone's responsibility?
- Has anyone checked that the equipment, tools or machines are right for the job?
- Are safe ways of doing the job already in place?
- Could this job interfere with the health and safety of others?

- Are safe working procedures laid down for the job. Is there any guidance which may help?
- Have people been trained and instructed in the use and limitations of the equipment?
- If the job cannot be finished today, can it be left in a safe state?
- Are clear instructions available for the next shift?
- Are the production people aware of what the maintenance staff are doing and vice versa?
- What might go wrong, e.g. accident, explosion, food poisoning, electrocution, fire, release of radioactivity, chemical spill?

### Permits to Work

Simple instructions or lock-off procedures are adequate for most jobs, but some require extra care. A 'permit to work' states exactly what work is to be done and when, and which parts are safe. A responsible person should assess the work and check safety at each stage. The people doing the job sign the permit to show that they understand the risk and precautions necessary. An example of a permit to work is given in Figure 12.1

Examples of high-risk jobs where a permit to work procedure may need to be used include:

- entry into vessels, confined spaces or machines;
- hot work which may cause explosion or fire;
- construction work or the use of contractors;
- cutting into pipework carrying hazardous substances;
- mechanical or electrical work requiring isolation of the power source, e.g. before work inside large machines, if locking off is not good enough;
- work on plant, boilers, mixers etc. which must be effectively cut off from the possible entry of fumes, gas, liquid or steam;
- testing for dangerous fumes or lack of oxygen before entering an unventilated pit or silo;
- vacuuming the inside of an empty grain silo to remove dust which might explode, before hot cutting a hole in the side.

### Lock-off Procedures

Before working on plant or equipment, isolate machines from the main power supply by locking off the power. Usually this is done by using a separate electrical switch.

**DETAILS OF PROPOSED WORK**

Intended start date:     Intended start time:     Expected duration:

CLEARANCE
Clearance is given for this work to take place:
Signature:     Position:     Date:

**CHECKLIST     SERVICE**
Electricity
Steam
Water
Gas
Compressed air
Hydraulics
Other services

**ISOLATIONS MADE**

**CHECKLIST**
Confined space     Radiation
Flammables     Access
Toxic substances     PPE
Lack of oxygen     Other

**OTHER PRECAUTIONS**

**RESTRICTIONS ON WORK**

**ISSUE**
I confirm the isolations and other pre-cautions described above have been carried out. I am satisfied the permit holder understands the restrictions on the work. **The permit is issued.**
Signature

Permit issuer

Date:     Time:

**WORK TERMINATION**
The work described above has terminated. All persons and equipment under my control are clear of the area which has been left in a safe condition.
Signature

Permit holder

Date:     Time:

**ACCEPTANCE**
I accept this permit to carry out the work described. I understand the restrictions described above and all persons under my control will abide by them.
Signature

Permit holder

Date:     Time:

**CANCELLATION**
**This permit is cancelled.** All isolations may be removed. Other precautions may cease. Normal activities may then resume.

Signature

Authorized person

Date:     Time:

Figure 12.1: Permit to work

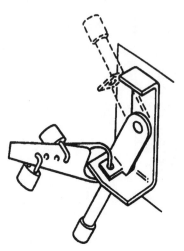

Figure 12.2: Use of multiple hasp

- Use a safety lock with only one key.
- Where several people are working, use a multiple hasp so that everyone can fit their own lock (See Figure 12.2).
- Only when all the locks have been removed can the equipment be switched on.
- Put a warning notice or label on the switch, and make sure it is removed when the work has finished.

## Check the Systems

You cannot rely on your systems always being right. Check that your rules and procedures not only deal with all the risks but are also being followed – particularly if people are working outside normal hours with less supervision than usual.

- Are all the risks covered?
- Do people follow procedures and do they have any ideas for improvements?
- Do you ask them?
- Are there any training gaps?
- Is the level of supervision right?

## Emergency Procedures

When things go wrong, people may be exposed to serious and immediate danger. Special procedures may be necessary for such emergencies as:

- **Fire.** Most employers have formalized fire procedures, often as a result of the requirements of their fire certificates.
- **Bomb threats.** This is a risk which has increased considerably in recent years, particularly for those in the public sector.
- **Hazardous substances.** Leaks or discharges of substances in their liquid or gaseous form are most likely to present serious and imminent danger.
- **Process problems.** Problems within industrial processes could also create situations of serious and imminent danger.
- **Power failure.** This could be the cause of process problems or could create dangers through the loss of ventilation equipment or lighting.
- **Violence.** This is another risk that is on the increase. The need for an emergency procedure should be considered whenever staff deal with the general public, especially in situations of potential conflict, e.g. complaints desks.
- **Crowds.** Even peaceful crowds can create situations of serious and imminent danger. Those in entertainment and sport will need to consider these risks.
- **Animals.** All animals including farm and domestic animals could cause danger to those working with them. This is particularly so if the animal is in a distressed state.
- **Weather.** Severe weather in the form of wind, rain, snow, extremes of temperature or lightning could result in unstable buildings, unsafe scaffolding, flooding, hypothermia etc.

## Emergency Plan

If a major incident at the workplace could involve risks to the public, rescuing employees or co-ordination of emergency services an emergency plan should be written.

Emergency procedures should include the following points:

- What action the person discovering the emergency is expected to take. How others are to be alerted to the emergency, and what action they should then take.

- Consider what might happen and how the alarm will be raised. Don't forget night and shift working, weekends and times when the premises are closed, e.g. holidays.
- Plan what to do, including how to call the emergency services. Assist the emergency services by clearly marking the premises from the road. Draw up a simple plan marked with the location of hazardous items.
- If more than 25 tonnes of dangerous substances are held the fire authority must be notified and warning signs put up (see Further Reading).
- Decide where to go to reach a place of safety or to get rescue equipment. Provide emergency lighting if necessary.
- Make sure there are enough emergency exits for everyone to escape quickly, and keep emergency doors and escape routes unobstructed and clearly marked.
- Nominate competent persons to take control.
- Decide who the other key people are, e.g. first aiders.
- Plan essential actions such as emergency plant shut-down or making processes safe. Important items such as shut-off valves and electrical isolators should be clearly labelled.
- Train everyone in emergency procedures. Don't forget the needs of people with disabilities.

*Further reading*
Dangerous Substances (Notification and Marking of Sites) Regulations 1990

## Reporting Injuries and Other Events

The Reporting of Injuries, Diseases and Dangerous Occurrences Regulations 1995 (RIDDOR) apply to all employers and the self-employed and cover everyone at work. The reporting action is as follows:

*Death or Major Injury*
If there is an accident connected with work and:

- an employee, or a self-employed person working on the premises is killed or suffers a major injury (including as a result of physical violence); or
- a member of the public is killed or suffers injuries which result in hospitalization;

the enforcing authority must be notified immediately, normally by telephone. They will ask for brief details about your business, the injured person and the accident. Within ten days this must be followed up with a completed accident report form, F2508 (see Figure 12.3, p. 92).

Definitions of major injuries can be found in the pad of report forms and is reproduced in Appendix D.

### Over-three-day Injury

If there is an accident connected with work (including an act of physical violence) and an employee, or a self-employed person working on the premises, suffers an over-three-day injury, a completed F2508 must be sent to the enforcing authority within ten days. An over-three-day injury is one which is not major but results in the injured person being away from work or unable to do their normal work for more than three days (including non-work days).

### Disease

If a doctor notifies an employer that an employee suffers from a reportable work-related disease then a completed disease report form, F2508A (see Figure 12.4, p. 93) must be sent to the enforcing authority. A summary of the reportable diseases is given in Appendix D. A full list is included with the pad of report forms and in the guide to the Regulations.

### Dangerous Occurrence

If something happens which does not result in a reportable injury, but which clearly could have done, then it may be a dangerous occurrence which must be reported immediately (e.g. by telephone). This must be followed up within ten days with a completed F2508. A summary of reportable dangerous occurrences is given in Appendix D. A full list is included with the pad of report forms and in the guide to the Regulations.

## Reporting

In general, reports should be made to the environmental health department of the local authority if the business is:

- office-based;
- retail or wholesale;
- warehousing;
- hotel and catering;
- sports or leisure;
- residential accommodation, excluding nursing homes;
- concerned with places of worship.

Figure 12.3: Form F2508

Figure 12.4: Form 2508A

For all other types of business it will be the area office of the HSE. The telephone number should be in the telephone directory under HSE.

## Keeping Records

A record must be kept of any reportable injury, disease or dangerous occurrence. This must include the date and method of reporting; the date, time and place of the event; personal details of those involved; and a brief description of the nature of the event or disease. The record can be kept in any form: for example, by keeping copies of the completed report forms in a file or recording the details on a computer.

*Further reading*
HSE: Everyone's guide to RIDDOR 1995, HSE31.
HSE: Reporting under RIDDOR, HSE24.
HSE: Your firm's injury records and how to use them, IND(G)113(L).

## First Aid

There must be:

- someone who can take charge in an emergency. An appointed person must be available whenever people are at work;
- a first-aid box;
- notices telling people where the first-aid box is and who the appointed person is;
- a trained first-aider and a first-aid room if the work gives rise to special hazards, e.g. using a particularly toxic material.

As the company grows, the need for qualified first-aiders should be reviewed. They must have the right training and are given a certificate valid for three years – after that a refresher course and re-examination are necessary. Training organisations are registered with EMAS.

*Further reading*
Health and Safety (First Aid) Regulations 1981.
HSE: First aid at work: general guidance for inclusion in first aid boxes, IND(G)4 (Rev.)(P).

## Investigating Events

When an accident happens:

- take any action required to deal with the immediate risk, e.g. first aid, put out fire, isolate any danger, fence off the area;
- assess the amount and kind of investigation needed – if the site has to be disturbed, photographs and measurements should be taken first;
- investigate – find out what happened and why;
- take steps to stop something similar happening again;
- also look at near misses and property damage. Often it is only by chance that someone wasn't injured.

### Checklist

To help with the investigation, find out:

- details of injured personnel;
- details of injury, damage or loss;
- the worst that could have happened and if it could happen again;
- if the standards were in place for the premises, plant, substances and procedures involved;
- if they were adequate and followed;
- if people were up to the job. Were they competent, trained and instructed?
- what was the underlying cause? Was there more than one?
- what was meant to happen and what the plans were. How were the people organized?
- if inspection would have picked up the problem earlier;
- if it had happened before. If so, why weren't the lessons learnt?

Most accidents have more than one cause so don't be too quick to blame individuals – try to deal with root causes.

# CHAPTER 13

# Personal Safety

## Healthcare

More people die from work-related diseases than from workplace incidents. Regulation 5 of the Management of Health and Safety at Work Regulations 1992 (MHSW) requires health surveillance under certain circumstances. Health surveillance is not required for most workers, but if there are known risks from the work carried out advice should be sought from the Employment Medical Advisory Service (EMAS) of the HSE. Health surveillance means having a system to look for early signs of ill-health caused by substances and other hazards at work. It includes keeping health records for individuals, and may include medical examinations so that corrective action can be taken.

There are other areas of healthcare which are of concern to employers:

### Eyecare

Regulation 5 of the Health and Safety (Display Screen Equipment) Regulations 1992 gives employers a duty to ensure the provision of appropriate eye and eyesight tests to existing and new employees who are 'users':

- on request;
- at regular intervals after the first test as recommended by an optometrist.

In addition, the Regulation requires employers to pay for 'special' corrective appliances (normally spectacles) to correct vision defects at the viewing distance or distances used specifically for the display screen work concerned. [A 'user' is defined as an employee who habitually uses display screen equipment as a significant part of his normal work.]

### Mental health or stress

Many people suffer some form of mental health problem at some time, and it is a significant reason for absence from work. Whilst work can have a beneficial effect on mental health, it can also bring worries. Too little personal control over work, not being allowed to use one's skills fully, being overworked or underworked, and boring work can all contribute to stress. Managers should learn to recognize the signs of stress and encourage employees to discuss problems openly. Help may only be needed in the form of sympathetic reassurance or practical advice, but in appropriate cases counselling or psychiatric help may be needed.

### Drugs and alcohol

Abuse of alcohol, drugs and other substances can affect work performance and safety. Again, managers should learn to recognize the signs and encourage workers to seek help. If strict standards are needed because of safety-critical jobs, the procedures should be agreed in advance with the workforce. Disciplinary action may be needed where safety is critical.

### Passive smoking

This is breathing in other people's tobacco smoke. Medical research indicates that passive smoking (or active for that matter!) can damage health, make asthma worse and, in extreme cases, cause lung cancer. Managers should agree some rules with the workforce to protect non-smokers; possibly by providing a smoke-free workplace or separate break areas. Any rest-rooms or rest areas must be arranged to avoid discomfort to non-smokers.

### Further reading

HSE: Surveillance of people exposed to health risks at work, HS(G)61.
HSE: Mental health at work, IND(G)59(L).
HSE: Protecting your health at work, IND(G)62(L).
HSE: Passive smoking at work, IND(G)63(L) (Rev.).
HSE: Need advice on occupational health?, IND(G)74(L).
HSE: What your doctor needs to know, IND(G)116(L).
HSE: Mental distress at work: first aid measures, IND(G)129(L).


## Personal Protective Equipment (PPE)

MHSW requires employers to identify and assess risks to health and safety present in the workplace, so enabling the most appropriate means of reducing those risks to an acceptable level. There is in effect a hierarchy of control measures, and PPE should always be regarded as the last resort to protect against risks to safety and health. Engineering controls and safe systems of work should always be considered first. There are a number of reasons for this approach:

- PPE protects only the person wearing it, whereas measures controlling the risk at source can protect everyone at the workplace;
- theoretical maximum levels of protection are seldom achieved with PPE in practice, and the actual level of protection is difficult to assess. Effective protection is only achieved by suitable PPE, correctly fitted, maintained and properly used;
- PPE may restrict the wearer by limiting mobility or visibility, or by requiring additional weight to be carried.

The Personal Protective Equipment at Work Regulations 1992 give the full requirements for PPE. In order to provide PPE for their employees, employers must do more than simply have the equipment on the premises. The equipment must be readily available or, at the very least, have clear instructions on where it can be obtained. By virtue of Section 9 of HASWA, no charge can be made to the worker for the provision of PPE which is used only at work.

In the selection and use of PPE, the employer must:

- consider – who is exposed and to what, for how long, and to how much;
- choose good quality products made to a recognized standard – suppliers can advise;
- choose equipment which suits the wearer – consider size, fit and weight. If the user helps to choose it, he may be more likely to wear it!
- make sure it fits properly – note in particular the problem of creating a good seal if a respirator user has a beard;
- make sure that if more than one item of PPE is to be worn they are compatible, e.g. a respirator may not give proper protection if air leaks in around the seal because the user is wearing safety glasses;
- instruct and train people in the use of PPE. Explain why it is needed, when to use it and its limitations;
- ensure that the equipment is properly looked after and stored when not in use. It must be cleaned and kept in good repair.

*Further reading*

HSE: Guidance on the Personal Protective Equipment at Work Regulations 1992, L25.
HSE: Guidance on the Construction (Head Protection) Regulations 1989.
HSE: Respiratory protective equipment: a practical guide for users, HS(G)53.

## Capabilities and Training

Regulation 11 of MHSW requires that employers take the employee's capabilities into account when entrusting tasks to them, and provide adequate health and safety training. The following is taken from the ACOP issued under the Regulation:

### Training

Training is an important way of achieving competence and helps to convert information into safe working practices. It contributes to the organization's health and safety culture and is needed at all levels, including top management. The risk assessment will help determine the level of training needed for each type of work as part of the preventative and protective measures. This can include basic skills training, specific on-the-job training and training on health and safety or emergency procedures.

Training needs are likely to be greatest on recruitment. New employees should receive basic induction training on health and safety, including arrangements for first aid, fire and evacuation. Particular attention should be given to the needs of young workers. The risk assessment should indicate further specific training needs. In some cases, training may be required even though an employee holds formal qualifications.

Changes in an employee's work environment may cause them to be exposed to new or increased risks, requiring further training. The need for further training should be considered when:

- employees transfer or take on new responsibilities. There may be a change in the work activity or in the work environment;
- there is a change in the work equipment or systems of work in use. A significant change is likely to need a review and reassessment of risks, which may indicate additional training needs. If the change includes introducing completely new technology, it may bring with it new and unfamiliar risks. Competent outside advice may be needed.

### Refresher training

An employee's competence will decline if skills (e.g. in emergency procedures) are not used regularly. Training therefore needs to be repeated periodically to ensure continued competence. Information from personal performance monitoring, health and safety checks, accident investigations and near-miss incidents can help to establish a suitable period for retraining. Special attention should be given to employees who occasionally deputize for others. Their skills are likely to be under-developed and they may need more frequent refresher training.

### Adaptation/working hours

Changes in risks may also require changes in the content of training, e.g. where new procedures have been introduced. Health and safety training should take place during working hours. If it is necessary to arrange training outside an employee's normal hours, this should be treated as an extension of time at work.

### Further reading

HSE: Mind how you go, IND(G)2(L)(Rev.).

# CHAPTER 14

# Communicating

Health and safety has to be communicated to all personnel in the company; either upwards to the policy-makers for decisions, or downwards to the workers for implementation. Communications about safety, whether upwards or downwards, are likely to be similar as they mostly concern the identification and avoidance of hazards. Managers can communicate their information either aurally or visually. Speech is obviously the most natural and direct method and is likely to be used whenever the message has to be relayed quickly. Management briefings are most easily given by speaking directly to employees; this also has the advantage of allowing the employees to ask questions to clarify areas of doubt or lack of understanding. However, the spoken word is lost once the briefing is over, whereas written communications convey their meaning indefinitely. In practice, the spoken word backed up by the written one will probably give the highest rate of understanding and retention.

A breakdown of widely-used methods of spoken and written communication follows, with acknowledgement to Tony Corfield's book *Safety Management*.

## Written Communications

### The written report

A frequently-met form of the upward decision-making communication is the written report. Specialist health and safety advisers normally use this form when proposing to line managers that adjustments should be made to the safety system. They may well raise the issue orally first, but if it is a matter of any substance, the oral statement needs to be backed up in writing. It would be wrong to assume that local managers, particularly those at the bottom end of the line, do not have to use the same form. Any one of them is likely to, for example, after an accident in his own area of responsibility. A written report is required: by management to help prevent a recurrence;

**INTRODUCTION**

Copies to:

TITLE IN CAPITALS

Identifying details: names, places, dates

From:

To:

| | |
|---|---|
| Introductory paragraph (unless routine report) | – why report came to be written and its purpose |

**BODY OF THE REPORT**

| | | |
|---|---|---|
| 1. | The situation | – the relevant facts |
| 2. | Analysis | – what are the dangers/opportunities |
| 3. | Selecting the most effective remedy/best course of action | |
| 4. | Action necessary | – *who* does *what, how, when* and *where*, and *cost*, where relevant |
| | *Appendices* | – as appropriate |

**CLOSING SECTION**

Signed

Status

Date

Figure 14.1: Framework for a written report

by HSE under the RIDDOR Regulations; by the insurance company; and by the company's solicitor as the basis for evidence should there be a civil law claim from an injured employee.

Reports proposing changes in the safety system need to be in writing because they are part of the decision-making process. The written form ensures that a durable record remains. In safety issues, where human life may be at stake, responsibility needs to be unambiguously assigned. The written communication in some measure binds the sender and the receiver. They are both personally designated in it. This is why it is essential that copies of all reports are filed away for subsequent reference.

*A recognized form*
For drafting management reports there is a recognized basic framework, though it does not have to be followed slavishly. The body of the report has to be bracketed between an introduction and a closing section.

- **Introduction.** The introduction sets out briefly the subject of the report, and should consist of a title, brief explanation of the issue and, where relevant, the date. The title should be set out at the head of the report and underlined. Underneath the title should follow the name of the author of the report, his authority, and the person to whom it is addressed. If the report is not routine, a short introductory paragraph may be needed to explain its purpose.
- **Main body of the report.** Next follows the substance of the report. This, if it is to be coherent, must proceed logically from stage to stage. It should be divided into some three or four related sections. There may be more or fewer depending on the nature and purpose of the report. But whatever their number, they should develop logically from one to another.
- **Closing section.** The closing section consists simply of the signature of the writer, his position in the company and the date.

*Four-step method.* If the main body of the report were to be patterned on the four-step problem-solving method, it would have the structure as set out in Figure 14.1. In practice, many of the reports on safety in a company tend to be based on this pattern. They deal with threatened or actual safety breakdowns in some facet or other of the system of work. This is, of course, the type which includes accident reports. A safety manager in a factory in which a serious accident has occurred would have to report on it to higher management. His report would be likely to follow this pattern:

- describe the accident;
- attempt to determine what caused it;
- prescribe a remedy;
- set out what action is needed to apply the remedy and prevent a reccurrence.

This is the system maintenance function. A report about an observed hazard at work as an example of its use in system maintenance follows. A method of assessing the value of a written report is given in Figure 14.2.

---

A report may be assessed from these standpoints:

1.  **Style**

    Clearly written and presented?

        – short sentences, correctly spelt, simple language.

    Courteous?

        – be careful about appearing heavy-handed.

---

2.  **Sense**

    Accurate?

    Relevant?

    Nothing essential omitted?

---

3.  **Structure**

    Clearly structured?

    | | |
    |---|---|
    | Introduction | – tuned in correctly? Title, names, dates, copies. |
    | Argument | – points logically linked, leading to action? |
    | Appendices | – where appropriate. |
    | Closing section | – signed, dated, authority? |

---

Figure 14.2: Assessing the value of a written report

*Example of a written report*

ELSBURY STORE – LIFT TRUCKS
IMPROPERLY PARKED ON GRADIENT 15 MAY 1996

*Report by:*
J. Planter, Safety Adviser, Brinham Plastics Plc.

*To:*
G. Entwhistle, Superintendent, Elsbury Store, Brinham Plastics Plc.

**The hazard**
At 1430 hrs on 15 May 1996 I observed two parked and unattended lift trucks on a steep gradient outside the canteen. Neither had chocks on the wheels. Any tampering with the brakes of these vehicles could have released the trucks on a one-in-ten gradient.

**Rules broken**
Parking the trucks on a gradient was a breach of the company's *Employee Safe Practices Handbook*, Section 18b, and therefore a breach of contract. It was also a breach of the HSE Guidance Booklet, *Safety in Working with Lift Trucks*, HS(G)6. This is not in itself a legal requirement, but failure to act on the guidance might lead to prosecution under the 1974 Health and Safety at Work Act. Section 2 could be used against the employer, and Section 7 against the operatives and the management staff.

**Proposals for removing the hazard**
a. Review the particular aspect of safety of internal transport at the Elsbury Store, and
b. consider the wider issue of educating staff and operators about the Company's employee safe practices by:
   i) briefing sessions on each of the main sections of the handbook;
   ii) a short course for supervisory staff to conduct the briefing sessions.

**Next step**
As agreed, I will visit the store again on 6 June 1996. We can then discuss the particular problem of internal transport and the larger principle of systematic briefing for the employees throughout the store.

*J. Planter*
*Safety Adviser, Brinham Plastics Plc*
*16 May 1996*

### The safety bulletin

The safety bulletin is an in-house publication posted on the noticeboard or circulated direct to employees. It possesses one advantage over the glossies produced by RoSPA and the British Safety Council: it deals with local problems and local people. The centrepiece of every publication should focus on an event which has happened inside the company, a person who is well known, or an issue which could directly affect the reader. Accidents and near-misses should be the staple news items. Individual reports can be written on each particular event. The trend of accidents can be described visually by graphics. There is also an abundance of standard material available covering wider issues. The HSE produces a constant flow of bulletins, newsletters and leaflets for this purpose. Other rich sources are produced by RoSPA, the British Safety Council, the Fire Prevention Association and even the national press. As the safety bulletin is not a commercial publication, the question of copyright should not arise from taking extracts from these publications. However, as a matter of courtesy one ought to seek permission first and acknowledge the source.

### Safety posters

Posters, used properly, can fulfil a propaganda role for safety managers. Used in isolation they may not have the desired effect, but as part of co-ordinated campaign posters can put a sharper edge on the message. Safety posters are professionally produced and often visually striking. Some of them use humour to get the message across (see Figure 14.3). The effectiveness of a poster depends on its dramatic impact and an element of surprise. It follows then that a particular poster should not be left on display for too long or the impact will be lost.

### Safety notices

From time to time special alerts have to be given to warn the workforce of new or unexpected hazards. Once the safety manager has spread the warning by word of mouth, a notice will be needed to reinforce the message. The notice should convey clearly and unambiguously the action to be taken. If the warning is going to be read, and not be lost amongst the plethora of other notices, it must stand out. Most managers these days have access to a word-processor so the opportunities exist to make the notice visually striking.

Figure 14.3: A safety poster

## Verbal Communications

The cogency and impact of all types of communication depend on the content and structure. In a spoken report the level to which the audience absorbs the information depends upon the presentation. For a start, it has to be delivered audibly and clearly. Next, it has to persuade. For this, a courteous and friendly tone is helpful, if not essential. Safety managers may, on occasion, have to draw attention to the safety laws. They should take care not to give the impression that they, themselves, are laying down the law. People tend to respond better to safety matters when persuaded rather than told.

### The spoken report

The opportunity for giving a spoken report may occur infrequently for most managers, but should be almost routine for the safety specialist. In companies which operate a safety committee, the specialist's report is likely to be the central item of business. Senior management may require a report on special hazards or any new Regulations which may affect the company.

The main outline of a spoken report is similar to that of a written report – they have the same internal logic. But a spoken report needs some modifications because special care is necessary to hold the attention of the audience. A written report can be picked up, put down for a cup of coffee, and picked up again for a second reading. A spoken report is a non-stop performance. The attention of the audience must be gained at the start and held to the very end.

The structure of an oral report is given in Figure 14.4. The introduction is used to tune the audience in to the subject matter and to grab their attention. Sometimes the subject matter itself is an attention-getter, e.g. an accident at the factory. If not, the speaker may need to highlight the relevance and importance. For example, in introducing a report on cadmium the speaker could explain 'I am going to talk to you about one of the metals we use in our factory. Among its many interesting qualities is one that concerns all of us – it is suspected of being a cancer-forming agent.' Having got the audience's attention, one of the best ways of keeping it is to make sure that they do not lose the thread of the argument in the body of the report. Thus, the main stages should be signposted in the introduction, and the transition between stages emphasised. To ensure that the audience goes away impressed, the speaker needs to conclude with a brief summary. One again, the audience has to be reminded how the issue affects them personally. Then the report should end with a punchline – a final sentence to make them sit up before they get up. An example of an oral report follows. A method of assessing the value of an oral report can be found in Figure 14.5 (p. 113).

---

**INTRODUCTION**

     Name and authority for speaking

     Subject – merely the title, and what is its importance for the audience

     Signposts – main points in the argument and their order

---

**MAIN BODY OF REPORT**

1.    Hazard/situation

     Supporting facts and argument

2.    Causes of hazard/opportunities

     Supporting facts and argument

3.    Remedy/method of seizing opportunities

     Supporting facts and argument

4.    Action needed

     Who does what, when, where, how, and if relevant, cost

---

**CONCLUSION**

     Brief summary, stressing the importance to the audience

     End on a punchline

---

Figure 14.4: Framework for an oral report

*Example of a short oral report*

– given by a safety adviser to a meeting of a safety committee (signposts to the structure are shown in brackets).

(Introduction)

My name is John Planter and, as most of you know, I am the safety adviser for Brinham Plastics. It's my pleasure to give you a report on the one-day conference I recently attended with the company's senior safety representative, Bill Meadows. It was held on 1st April this year at Birmingham University's Manor House, an ex-Cadbury mansion in beautiful parkland on the edge of the city. The title of the conference was 'The third decade of the 1974 Health and Safety at Work Act – Which way forward?' As to its importance, I need only list the speakers: David Eyres is the HSE's Chief Inspector of Factories; David Thornbury is our Area Director for the HSE; and Dr Cedric Thompson is one of the CBI's nominees on the Health and Safety Commission. They are the three front-row forwards in the safety pack.

I would like to take the sections of my report in the following order: First, the message the conference gave us; second, what their message could mean for the company; third, what tactics seem to be called for from our safety committee; and fourth, to decide with you our immediate action.

(Stage 1 )

First, what was the case made by the platform speakers?

They all made it clear there is not going to be a lot of change in the national safety scheme, at least over the next ten years. The flow of new legislation, once Regulations in the pipeline were cleared, would pretty well dry up. We would have a stable framework of law within which to work. There is unlikely to be a big increase in manpower in the inspectorates, so the inspectors will not have time for more routine workplace inspections. Their conclusion was that firms will have to rely more upon themselves. They will have to draw upon the store of technical and professional skill already available within industry and the insurance companies. In future, the emphasis should be placed more firmly upon self-regulation – to help set standards and monitor them. But self-regulation should not just be regarded as calling in experts. The speakers emphasised the primary importance of strengthening management. This was not just in planning and organizing a safe system, but in controlling it as well. All the speakers played on the theme of self-help.

In answering questions from the delegates they merely amplified the same case. How, they were asked, would the policy of self-regulation work with small businesses, particularly in the construction industry? The delegates mentioned firms with no safety professionals of their own, who were not members of any trade association, and none of whose employees had any links with a trade union to put management under pressure from safety representatives. The platform speaker's reply was that, if the big firms could be relied upon to look after themselves by self-regulation, inspectors would be freed to concentrate on the small firms.

That about sums up their message for us. Now may I outline, for my second step, what the message might mean for the company?

(Stage 2 )

It seems clear that the HSE will pursue their policy of self-regulation for safety at work. It does not seem likely that all this drum-banging is for nothing!

The outcome seems to be that the HSE will be encouraging the bigger companies to produce safety policies which demonstrate self-assessment. They will look for evidence in them of systematic monitoring and assessment backed by professional specialists either from within the firm or from outside. Above all, they will look for positive management control over them. So what does this mean for the company? We are an obvious candidate for self-regulation. We already have a safety scheme, comprehensive safety codes, a safety committee, safety training at all levels, and a system of safety inspections. We are likely, therefore, to come under the spotlight. The inspectors are likely to look to us to set an example. This is surely the message for us.

(Stage 3 )

My next step is to consider what we as a safety committee have to do in order to respond to the challenge. If the company is going to be able to demonstrate that we have a self-sufficient safety system, every aspect of it will have to be critically reviewed. It will have to be studied both in terms of effectiveness and cost. We must have detailed analyses from our chemists and occupational health staffs as to how health standards are maintained and audited. We will need a separate session with the fire prevention officer about fire control. Then there are the responsibilities of security and environmental hazards, as well as our general standards of plant and workplace safety. Finally, we will need to keep in touch with the factory inspector. Where better to get an opinion on what the form is than out of the horse's mouth?

(Stage 4 )

That sums up the response we ought to be considering. It brings me to my final step. What immediate action is called for from us? I have discussed the next move with Bill Meadows. He has agreed to second the proposal I shall now put forward. It is that this safety committee recommends to the managing director that the company conducts a systematic survey of our safety systems on the lines that I have outlined.

(Conclusion)

Before handing over to Bill, may I briefly wind up my report. The HSE are giving us the plainest of hints we have got to make ouselves self-reliant in safety. As a safety committee we can give the company a lead on this. We are often accused of being over-ready to press the brake pedal – so let's give them a touch of the accelerator!

### Safety briefing

The safety briefing is a method of alerting attention to the key elements in a safety code or safety problem. Where possible, the spoken briefing should be reinforced by the use of visual media. A safety briefing needs to be relevant in its content, and this content has to be designed in such a way that it can be readily assimilated. A third requirement is that it should be presented attractively. Its presentation must be good enough first to alert attention and then to maintain it – some employees are not all that readily turned on to safety issues!

A suggested method for the safety brief is in Figure 14.6 (p. 114).

### Further reading

*Safety Management* by Tony Corfield.

A report may be assessed from three standpoints:

## STYLE

Clear?

- no irritating mannerisms: 'ums', ers'

- no repetitive 'basicallys' and 'you knows'

Friendly?

Persuasive?

- sound as though you mean it

- choose examples which are useful and interesting

## SENSE

Accurate?

Relevant?

Nothing essential omitted?

## STRUCTURE

Clearly structured?

Introduction

- who you are, authority for speaking

- focusing attention on subject

- signposting the route

Elements logically related?

- each led in clearly

Conclusion

- summary

- re-stress relevance to audience

- don't fade out – finish on a high note

Figure 14.5: Assessing the value of an oral report

**Introduction**

Alert interest; give topic and stress importance to the individuals present

**Getting it across**

- Itemize and explain each group of up to four points.

- Get the points discussed by employees, e.g. ask them individually what their experience is.
Get them to give examples from what they have seen or done themselves in the workplace.
- Question each individual to ensure the points have been understood.

**Winding up**

Emphasise the action required

Go out on a strong note

Figure 14.6: A safety brief

# CHAPTER 15

# Managing the Policy

So, we now understand how health and safety law affects us; we have written our health and safety policy statement; completed the risk assessment; and all the staff from the MD down are aware of their role and have received the required training. Time now to accept the plaudits from the boss, put the documentation on the shelf and move on to more pressing matters?

Well, not quite!

## Review and Audit

Regulation 3 of MHSW requires employers and the self-employed to review and, if necessary, amend their risk assessments, since assessment should not be a once-and-for-all activity. The nature of work changes, possibly affecting the associated hazards and risks. Monitoring of the health and safety policy, as required by Regulation 4 of MHSW, may reveal near-misses or defects in plant. Adverse events may take place even if a suitable and sufficient risk assessment has been made, and appropriate protective and preventative measures taken. The employer needs to review the risk assessment if there are developments that suggest that it may no longer be valid (or that it can be improved). In most cases, it is prudent to plan to review risk assessments at regular intervals – the time between reviews being dependent on the nature of the risks and the degree of change likely in the work activity. Such reviews should form part of standard management practice.

Remember! Things change: new materials come in; machines wear out, break down and need regular maintenance; rules get broken; and people don't always do as they are told. The only way to find out about changes like this is by checking. Don't wait until things have gone wrong. Do not try to check everything at once, but deal with a few key issues at a time, starting with the main hazards. This will not only let people know that checks will be made, but show that you are interested in what is happening in the workplace, not just when things go wrong.

Some important items may need checking daily, while others can safely be left much longer. Key examples are:

- ventilation plant must be examined and tested every 14 months;
- power press guards must be inspected during each shift;
- scaffolds must be inspected weekly;
- rescue equipment must be examined monthly.

Other periodic tests and examinations must be carried out by a competent person.

The rule should be: Act now to get control – don't react to an accident tomorrow!

## Five steps

In conclusion, and by way of a summary, I can do no better than to reproduce the contents of the HSE publication 'Five steps to successful health and safety management'.

### Why managing health and safety is important to you

Every working day in Great Britain two people are killed and over 6,000 are injured at work. Every year three quarters of a million people take time off work because of what they regard as work-related illness. Around 31 million work days are lost as a result.

Accidents and ill health are costly to workers and their families. They can also kill and cripple companies because, in addition to the costs of personal injuries, they may incur far greater costs of damage to property or equipment, and lost production. Only a small proportion of these are recoverable from insurance. Management control of health and safety is essential and is particularly important in smaller firms where fatal and major injury rates tend to be higher and the losses from a major accident can ruin the company.

Directors and managers can be held personally responsible for failures to control health and safety. Can you afford such failures? Do you really manage health and safety? What follows shows you how. It lists five steps to success. Following them will help you to keep your staff at work and reduce the costs of injuries, illness, property and equipment damage. You will have fewer production stoppages, higher output and better quality. By complying with the law and avoiding fines you will avoid damaging publicity. You cannot be a 'quality' organization unless you apply sound management principles to health and safety.

Inspectors visiting your workplace will want to know how you manage health and safety. If an accident occurs, your systems and procedures will come under scrutiny. Will they stand up to the examination? Read about the five steps and ask yourself the five questions after each one. Get your managers and staff to discuss them.

## Step 1: Set Your Policy

The same sorts of mistake that cause injuries and illness can also lead to property damage and interrupt production, so you must aim to control all accidental loss. Identifying hazards and assessing risks, deciding what precautions are needed, putting them in place and checking they are used protects people, improves quality, and safeguards plant and production. Your health and safety policy should influence all your activities, including the selection of people, equipment and materials, the way work is done and how you design goods and services. A written statement of your policy and the organization and arrangements for implementing and monitoring it shows your staff, and anyone else, that hazards have been identified and risks assessed, eliminated or controlled.

*Ask yourself:*
1. Do you have a clear policy for health and safety: is it written down?
2. Does it specify who is responsible, and the arrangements for identifying hazards, assessing risks and controlling them?
3. Do your staff know about the policy and understand it: are they involved in making it work?
4. Is it up to date?
5. Does it prevent injuries, reduce losses and really affect the way you work? Be honest!

## Step 2: Organize Your Staff

To make your health and safety policy effective you need to get your staff involved and committed. This is often referred to as 'health and safety culture'.

### Four 'Cs' of Health and Safety Culture

**Competence:** recruitment, training and advisory support.
**Control:** allocating responsibilities and securing commitment.
**Co-operation:** between individuals and groups.
**Communication:** verbal, written and visible.

### Competence

- Assess the skills needed to carry out all tasks safely.
- Provide the means to ensure that all employees, including temporary staff, are adequately instructed and trained.
- Ensure that people on especially dangerous work have the necessary training, experience and other qualities to carry the work out safely.
- Arrange for access to sound advice and help.

### Control

- Lead by example: demonstrate your commitment and provide clear direction.
- Identify people responsible for particular health and safety jobs – especially where special expertise is called for.
- Ensure that foremen and supervisors understand their responsibilities.
- Ensure all employees know what they must do and how they will be supervised and held accountable.

### Co-operation

- Consult your staff and their representatives.
- Involve them in planning and reviewing performance, writing procedures and solving problems.

### Communication

- Provide information about hazards, risks and preventative measures.
- Discuss health and safety regularly.

### Ask yourself:

1. Have you allocated responsibilities for health and safety to specific people?
2. Do you consult and involve your staff and the safety representatives effectively?
3. Do your staff have sufficient information about the risks they run and the preventative measures?

4. Do you have the right levels of expertise? Are your people properly trained?
5. Do you need specialist advice from outside the organization, and have you arranged to obtain it?

## Step 3: Plan and Set Standards

Planning is the key to ensuring that your health and safety efforts really work. Planning for health and safety involves setting objectives, identifying hazards, assessing risks, implementing standards of performance and developing a positive culture. It is often useful to record your plans in writing. Your planning should provide for:

- identifying hazards and assessing risks, and deciding how they can be eliminated or controlled;
- complying with the health and safety laws that apply to your business;
- agreeing health and safety targets with managers and supervisors;
- a purchasing and supply policy which takes health and safety into account;
- design of tasks, processes, equipment, products and services;
- safe systems of work;
- procedures to deal with serious and imminent danger;
- co-operation with neighbours and/or sub-contractors;
- setting standards against which performance can be measured.

Standards help to build a positive culture and control risks. They should identify who does what, when, and with what result, and apply to:

- premises, place of work and environmental control;
- plant and substances, purchase, supply, transport, storage and use;
- procedures, design of jobs and the way work is done;
- people, training and supervision;
- products and services, design, delivery, transport and storage.

*Three key points about standards*
They must be: measurable; achievable; realistic.

Statements such as 'staff must be trained' are difficult to measure if you don't know exactly what 'trained' means and who is to do the work. 'All machines will be guarded' is difficult to achieve if there is no measure of the adequacy of the guarding. Many industry-based standards already exist and you can adopt them where applicable. In other cases you will have to take advice and set your own, preferably referring to numbers, quantities and levels which are seen to be realistic and can be checked. For example:

- maintaining workshop temperature within a specific range;
- specifying levels of waste, effluent or emissions that are acceptable;
- methods and frequency for checking guards on machines;
- ergonomic design criteria for tasks and workstations;
- specific levels of training;
- agreements to consult staff or their representatives at specified intervals;
- monitoring performances in particular ways at specified times.

*Ask yourself:*
1. Do you have a health and safety plan?
2. Is health and safety always considered before any new work is started?
3. Have you identified hazards and assessed risks to your own staff and the public, and set standards for premises, plant, substances, procedures, people and products?
4. Do you have a plan to deal with serious or imminent danger, e.g. fires, process deviations etc?
5. Are the standards implemented and risks effectively controlled?

## Step 4: Measure Your Performance

Just like finance, production or sales, you need to measure your health and safety performance to find out if you are being successful. You need to know:

- where you are;
- where you want to be;
- what is the difference and why?

Active monitoring, before things go wrong, involves regular inspection and checking to ensure that your standards are being implemented and management controls are working. Reactive monitoring, after things go wrong, involves learning from your mistakes, whether they result in injuries and illness, property damage or near misses.

*Two key components of monitoring systems*
- *Active monitoring* (before things go wrong): Are you implementing the standards you set yourself and are they effective?
- *Reactive monitoring* (after things go wrong): Investigating injuries, cases of illness, property damage and near-misses – identifying in each case why performance was sub-standard.

You need to ensure that information from active and reactive monitoring is used to identify situations that create risks, and to do something about them. Priority should be given where risks are greatest. Look closely at serious events and those with potential for serious harm. Both require an understanding of the immediate and the underlying causes of events. Investigate and record what happened – find out why. Refer the information to the people with authority to take remedial action, including organizational and policy changes.

*Ask yourself:*
1. Do you know how well you perform in health and safety?
2. How do you know if you are meeting your own standards for health and safety?
3. How do you know you are complying with the health and safety laws that affect your business?
4. How great are your losses?
5. Do you have accurate records of injuries, ill health and accidental loss?

## Step 5: Learn From Experience: Audit and Review

Monitoring provides the information to enable you to review activities and decide how to improve performance. Audits, by your own staff or outsiders, complement monitoring activities by looking to see if your policy, organization and systems are actually achieving the right results. They tell you about the reliability and effectiveness of your systems. Learn from your experiences. Combine the results from measuring performance with information from audits to improve your approach to health and safety management. Review the effectiveness of your health and safety policy, paying particular attention to:

- the degree of compliance with health and safety performance standards (including legislation);
- areas where standards are absent or inadequate;

- achievement of stated objectives within given timescales;
- injury, illness and incident data: analyses of immediate and underlying causes, trends and common features.

These indicators will show you where you need to improve.

*Ask yourself:*
1. How do you learn from your mistakes?
2. Do you operate a health and safety audit system?
3. What action is taken on audit findings?
4. Does the audit involve staff at all levels?
5. When did you last review your policy and performance?

## Conclusion

This approach to managing health and safety is tried and tested. It has strong similarities to systems for total quality management used by many successful companies. It can help you to protect people and control loss. All five steps are fundamental. How well did you answer the questions about each step? If you think there is room for improvement, act today; don't react to an accident tomorrow.

## ONE FINAL POINT

You get the level of health and safety that you demonstrate you want. Health and safety is no accident; it has to be managed.

# References

**Further Reading**

*General*

*Essential Health and Safety for Managers*, Ron Akass, ISBN 0-566-07332-3.
*Health and Safety Survival Guide*, Terry Brimson, ISBN 0-07-709049-7.
*Safety Management*, Tony Corfield.

*Legislation*

The following publications can normally be obtained from HMSO:

Asbestos (Prohibitions) Regulations 1992.
Chemicals (Hazard Information and Packaging) CHIP Regulations 1993.
Construction (Design and Management) Regulations 1994.
Construction (Head Protection) Regulations 1989.
Control of Asbestos at Work Regulations 1987.
Control of Asbestos at Work (Amendment) Regulations 1992.
Control of Lead at Work Regulations 1980.
Control of Substances Hazardous to Health (COSHH) Regulations 1988 .
Control of Substances Hazardous to Health (Amendment) Regulations 1991 and 1992.
Dangerous Substances (Notification and Marking of Sites) Regulations 1990.
Electricity at Work Regulations 1989.
Employers' Liability (Compulsory Insurance) Act 1969.
Environmental Protection Act 1990.
Factories Act 1961.
Fire Precautions Act 1971.
Fire Precautions (Places of Work) Regulations 1995.
Food Hygiene (General) Regulations 1970.
Food Hygiene (Amendment) Regulations 1990 and 1991.
Food Safety Act 1990.
Health and Safety (Consultation with Employees) Regulations 1996.

Health and Safety (Display Screen Equipment) Regulations 1992.
Health and Safety (First Aid) Regulations 1981.
Health and Safety (Safety Signs and Signals) Regulations 1996.
Health and Safety at Work etc. Act 1974 .
The Ionising Radiations Regulations 1985.
Management of Health and Safety at Work Regulations 1992.
Manual Handling Operations Regulations 1992.
Noise at Work Regulations 1989.
Offices, Shops and Railway Premises Act 1963.
Personal Protective Equipment at Work Regulations 1992.
Power Presses Regulations 1965 and 1972.
Provision and Use of Work Equipment Regulations 1992.
Reporting of Injuries, Diseases and Dangerous Occurrences Regulations 1995.
Safety Representatives and Safety Committee Regulations 1977.
Woodworking Machines Regulations 1974.
Workplace (Health, Safety and Welfare) Regulations 1992.

## HSE Publications

The following list of HSE publications is just a small selection of those available. A comprehensive list is available from HSE Books. Leaflets and other items which are available free of charge from HSE area offices and HSE Books are marked with an asterisk *. In addition, HSE provides an autofax service for the most popular publications. Details can be found at the end of the list.

### Organizing for Safety
#### 1. Managing Health and Safety

|  | Essentials of Health and Safety at Work | ISBN 0-7176-0716-X |
|---|---|---|
| COP1 | Safety representatives and safety committees | ISBN 0-11-883959-4 |
| HS(G)65 | Successful health and safety management | ISBN 0-7176-0425-X |
| HS(G)96 | The costs of accidents at work | ISBN 0-7176-0439-X |
| L1 | A guide to the HSW Act | ISBN 0-7176-0441-1 |
| L21 | Management of Health and Safety at Work Regulations 1992. Approved Code of Practice | ISBN 0-7176-0412-8 |
| Poster | Health and safety law: What you should know | ISBN 0-11-701424-9 |
|  | Writing your health and safety policy statement: guide to preparing a safety policy statement for a small business | ISBN 0-7176-0424-1 |
|  | You can do it. The what, why and how of improving health and safety – a self-help guide | ISBN 0-7176-0726-7 |

| | | |
|---|---|---|
| HSC2 | HSW Act: the Act outlined | * |
| HSC3 | HSW Act: advice to employers | * |
| HSC5 | HSW Act: advice to employees | * |
| HSC6 | Writing a safety policy statement: advice to employers | * |
| HSC8 | Safety committees: guidance to employers whose employees are not members of recognised independent trade unions | * |
| HSE4(Rev.) | Employers' Liability (Compulsory Insurance) Act 1969: a short guide | * |
| HSE5(Rev.) | An introduction to the Employment Medical Advisory Service | * |
| HSE23(Rev.) | Health and safety legislation and trainees: a guide for employers | * |
| HSE25 | HSE and you | * |
| HSE26 | HSE – working with employers | * |
| IND(G)2(L) | Mind how you go! | * |
| IND(G)132(L) | Five steps to successful health and safety management: special help for directors and managers | * |
| IND(G)163(L) | Five steps to risk assessment | * |

## Premises
### 2. The Workplace

| | | |
|---|---|---|
| EH22 | Ventilation of the workplace | ISBN 0-11-885403-8 |
| HS(G)38 | Lighting at work | ISBN 0-7176-0467-5 |
| HS(G)55 | Health and safety in kitchens and food preparation areas | ISBN 0-11-885427-5 |
| HS(G)57 | Seating at work | ISBN 0-11-885431-3 |
| | Health and Safety in Engineering Workshops | ISBN 0-7176-0880-8 |
| HS(G)76 | Health and safety in retail and wholesale warehouses | ISBN 0-11-885731-2 |
| HS(G)104 | Health and safety in residential care homes | ISBN 0-7176-0673-2 |
| HS(G)105 | Health and safety in horse riding establishments | ISBN 0-7176-0632-5 |
| L24 | Workplace (Health, Safety and Welfare) Regulations 1992  Approved Code of Practice and guidance | ISBN 0-7176-0413-6 |
| L26 | Health and Safety (Display Screen Equipment) Regulations 1992 | ISBN 0-7176-0410-1 |
| | Guidance on Regulations Farm wise: your guide to health and safety | ISBN 0-11-882107-5 |
| IND(S)15(L) | Health and safety in small clothing factories | * |
| IND(G)36(L) | Working with VDUs | * |
| IND(G)184(L) | Signpost to the Health and Safety (Safety Signs and Signals) Regulations 1996 | * |
| HS(G)90 | VDUs: an easy guide to the Regulations | ISBN 0-7176-0735-6 |

### 3. Building Work

| | | |
|---|---|---|
| | Health and Safety in Construction | ISBN 0-7176-1143-4 |
| Form F91 Pt1 | Section A: Record of inspections of scaffolding | ISBN 0-7176-0437-3 |

| GS7 | Accidents to children on construction sites | ISBN 0-11-885416-X |
|---|---|---|
| GS15 | General access scaffolds | ISBN 0-11-883545-9 |
| GS25 | Prevention of falls to window cleaners | ISBN 0-11-885682-0 |
| GS28/1 | Safe erection of structures. Part 1: initial planning and design | ISBN 0-11-883584-X |
| GS28/2 | Safe erection of structures. Part 2: site management and procedures | ISBN 0-11-883605-6 |
| GS28/3 | Safe erection of structures. Part 3: working places and access | ISBN 0-11-883530-0 |
| GS28/4 | Safe erection of structures. Part 4: legislation and training | ISBN 0-11-883531-9 |
| GS29/1 | Health and safety in demolition work Part 1: preparation and planning | ISBN 0-11-885405-4 |
| GS29/3 | Health and safety in demolition work Part 3: techniques | ISBN 0-11-883609-9 |
| GS29/4 | Health and safety in demolition work Part 4: health hazards | ISBN 0-11-883604-8 |
| GS31 | Safe use of ladders, stepladders and trestles | ISBN 0-11-883594-7 |
| GS42 | Tower scaffolds | ISBN 0-11-883941-1 |
| HS(G)46 | A guide for small contractors. Site safety and concrete construction | ISBN 0-11-885475-5 |
| HS(G)47 | Avoiding danger from underground services | ISBN 0-7176-0435-7 |
| L22 | Provision and Use of Work Equipment Regulations 1992 Guidance on Regulations | ISBN 0-7176-0414-4 |
| L24 | Workplace (Health, Safety and Welfare) Regulations 1992 Approved Code of Practice and guidance | ISBN 0-7176-0413-6 |
| PM28 | Working platforms on forklift trucks | ISBN 0-11-883392-8 |
| PM30 | Suspended access equipment | ISBN 0-11-883577-7 |
| PM63 | Inclined hoists used in building and construction work | ISBN 0-11-883945-4 |
| | Deadly maintenance: roofs: a study of fatal accidents at work | ISBN 0-11-883804-0 |
| | Deadly maintenance: a study of fatal accidents at work | ISBN 0-11-883806-7 |
| | Safe working with small dumpers | ISBN 0-11-883693-5 |
| IND(G)55(P) | Bitumen boilers in construction – fire hazards | * |
| | Electrical Safety on Construction Sites | ISBN 0-7176-1000-4 |

## *Plant and Machinery*
## 4. Machinery Safety

| BS EN 292:1991 | Safety of machinery: Basic concepts, general principles for design | |
|---|---|---|
| BS 5304:1988 | Safety of machinery | |
| HS(G)17 | Safety in the use of abrasive wheels | ISBN 0-7176-0466-7 |
| HS(G)31 | Pie and tart machines | ISBN 0-11-883891-1 |
| HS(G)35 | Catering safety: food preparation machinery | ISBN 0-11-883910-1 |

| HS(G)42 | Safety in the use of metal cutting guillotines and shears | ISBN 0-11-885455-0 |
| HS(G)44 | Drilling machines: guarding of spindles and attachments | ISBN 0-7176-0616-3 |
| HS(G)45 | Safety in meat preparation: guidance for butchers | ISBN 0-11-885461-5 |
| HS(G)55 | Health and safety in kitchens and food preparation areas | ISBN 0-11-885427-5 |
| HS(G)89 | Safeguarding agricultural machinery: moving parts | ISBN 0-11-882051-6 |
| L2 | The Power Presses Regulations 1965 and 1972 | ISBN 0-11-885534-4 |
| L4 | Woodworking Machines Regulations 1974. Guidance on the Regulations | ISBN 0-11-885592-1 |
| L22 | Provision and Use of Work Equipment Regulations 1992. Guidance on Regulations | ISBN 0-7176-0414-4 |
| PM33 | Safety of bandsaws in the food industry | ISBN 0-11-883564-5 |
| PM35 | Safety in the use of reversing dough brakes | ISBN 0-11-883576-9 |
| PM65 | Worker protection at crocodile (alligator) shears | ISBN 0-11-883935-7 |
| PM66 | Scrap baling machines | ISBN 0-11-883936-5 |

## 5. Gas and Oil-Fired Equipment

| COP20 | Standards of training in safe gas installation | ISBN 0-11-883966-7 |
| HS(G)16 | Evaporating and other ovens | ISBN 0-11-883433-9 |

## 6. Plant and Equipment Maintenance

| HS(G)62 | Health and safety in tyre exhaust premises | ISBN 0-11-885594-8 |
| HS(G)67 | Health and safety in motor vehicle repair | ISBN 0-11-885671-5 |
| L22 | Provision and Use of Work Equipment Regulations 1992. Guidance on Regulations | ISBN 0-7176-0414-4 |
| L24 | Workplace (Health, Safety and Welfare) Regulations 1992 Approved Code of Practice and guidance | ISBN 0-7176-0413-6 |
| PM38 | Selection and use of electric handlamps | ISBN 0-11-886360-6 |
| PM55 | Safe working with overhead travelling cranes | ISBN 0-11-883524-6 |
| SWH428 | Inflation of tyres and removal of wheels (cautionary notice) | ISBN 0-11-880856-7 |
| | Deadly maintenance: a study of fatal accidents at work | ISBN 0-11-883806-7 |
| IND(G)50(C) | Safe use of petrol in garages | * |

## 7. Pressurized Plant and Systems

| COP37/38 | Pressure Systems and Transportable Gas Containers Regulations 1989 | ISBN 0-11-885514-X |
| GS4 | Safety in pressure testing | ISBN 0-11-886338-X |
| HS(G)39 | Compressed air safety | ISBN 0-11-885582-4 |
| HS(R)30 | A guide to the Pressure Systems and Transportable Gas Containers Regulations 1989 | ISBN 0-11-885516-6 |
| PM5 | Automatically controlled steam and hot water boilers | ISBN 0-11-885425-9 |
| PM29 | Electrical hazards from steam/water pressure cleaners etc. | ISBN 0-11-883538-6 |

| PM60 | Steam boiler blowdown systems | ISBN 0-11-883949-7 |
| | Pressure Systems and Transportable Gas Containers Regulations 1989: an open learning course | ISBN 0-7176-0687-2 |
| IND(G)68(L) | Do you use a steam/water pressure cleaner? | * |

## 8. Handling and Transporting

| COP | Safety of loads on vehicles (Department of Transport) (Available from HMSO) | ISBN 0-11-550666-7 |
| GS9 | Road transport in factories and similar workplaces | ISBN 0-11-885732-0 |
| GS39 | Training of crane drivers and slingers | ISBN 0-11-883932-2 |
| HS(G)6 | Safety in working with lift trucks | ISBN 0-11-886395-9 |
| HS(G)23 | Safety at power operated mast work platforms | ISBN 0-11-883820-2 |
| HS(G)60 | Work related upper limb disorders: a guide to prevention | ISBN 0-11-885565-4 |
| L23 | Manual Handling Operations Regulations 1992 Guidance on the Regulations | ISBN 0-7176-0411-X |
| L24 | Workplace (Health, Safety and Welfare) Regulations 1992 Approved Code of Practice and guidance | ISBN 0-7176-0413-6 |
| PM15 | Safety in the use of timber pallets | ISBN 0-11-882161-X |
| PM46 | Wedge and socket anchorages for wire ropes | ISBN 0-11-883611-0 |
| | Guidance on manual handling of loads in the health services | ISBN 0-7176-0430-6 |
| | Safe working with small dumpers | ISBN 0-11-883693-5 |
| IND(G)109(L) | Lighten the load: guidance for employers on muscoskeletal disorders | * |
| IND(G)125(L) | Handling and stacking bales in agriculture | * |
| IND(G)143(L) | Getting to grips with manual handling: a short guide for employers | * |
| IND(G)145(L) | Watch your back: avoiding back strain in timber handling and chainsaw work | * |
| IND(G)148(L) | Reversing vehicles | * |

## 9. Noise

| HS(G)56 | Noise at work: Noise guides 3 to 8 | ISBN 0-11-885430-5 |
| | Noise at work: Noise guides 1 and 2 | ISBN 0-7176-0454-3 |
| PM56 | Noise from pneumatic systems | ISBN 0-11-883529-7 |
| IND(G)75(L) | Introducing the Noise at Work Regulations | * |
| IND(G)99(L) | Noise at work: advice for employees | * |
| IND(G)127(L) | Noise in construction | |
| HS(G)138 | Sound Solutions – Techniques for Reducing Noise at Work | ISBN 0-7176-0791-7 |

## 10. Vibration

| HS(G)88 | Hand-arm vibration | ISBN 0-7176-0743-7 |
| IND(G)175(L) | Hand-arm vibration: Advice for employers | * |
| IND(G)126(L) | Hand-arm vibration: Advice on vibration white finger for employees and the self-employed | * |

## 11. Radiations

| | | |
|---|---|---|
| COP16 | Protection of persons against ionising radiation arising from any work activity: The Ionising Radiations Regulations 1985 | ISBN 0-7176-0508-6 |
| COP23 | Exposure to radon: The Ionising Radiations Regulations 1985 | ISBN 0-11-883978-0 |
| GS18 | Commercial ultraviolet tanning equipment | ISBN 0-11-883553-X |
| HS(G)91 | A framework for the restriction of occupational exposure to ionising radiation | ISBN 0-11-886324-X |
| L7 | Dose limitation – restriction of exposure. Approved Code of Practice | ISBN 0-11-885605-7 |
| L49 | Protection of outside workers against ionising radiations | ISBN 0-7176-0681-3 |
| Printing IAC | Safety in the use of inks, varnishes and lacquers cured by ultraviolet light or electron beam techniques | ISBN 0-11-882045-1 |
| IND(G)147(L) | Keep your top on | * |

## 12. Electricity

| | | |
|---|---|---|
| GS6 | Avoidance of danger from overhead electrical lines | ISBN 0-11-885668-5 |
| GS27 | Protection against electric shock | ISBN 0-11-883583-1 |
| GS47 | Safety of electrical distribution systems on factory premises | ISBN 0-11-885596-4 |
| GS50 | Electrical safety at places of entertainment | ISBN 0-11-885598-0 |
| HS(G)85 | Electricity at work: safe working practices | ISBN 0-7176-0442-X |
| HS(G)107 | Maintenance of portable and transportable electrical equipment | ISBN 0-7176-0715-1 |
| HS(R)25 | Memorandum of guidance on the Electricity at Work Regulations 1989 | ISBN 0-11-883963-2 |
| PM29 | Electrical hazards from steam/water pressure cleaners etc. | ISBN 0-11-883538-6 |
| PM32 | Safe use of portable electrical apparatus | ISBN 0-11-885590-5 |
| PM38 | Selection and use of electric handlamps | ISBN 0-11-886360-6 |
| PM64 | Electrical safety in arc welding | ISBN 0-7176-0704-6 |
| IND(G)139(L) | Electric storage batteries: safe charging and use | * |
| IND(G)159(L) | Maintaining portable electrical equipment in hotels and tourist accommodation | * |
| IND(G)160(L) | Maintaining portable electrical equipment in offices and other low-risk environments | * |

## *Substances*

## 13. Harmful Substances

| | | |
|---|---|---|
| COP2 | Control of lead at work | ISBN 0-11-883780-X |
| EH10 | Asbestos – exposure limits and measurement of airborne dust concentrations | ISBN 0-11-885552-2 |
| EH29 | Control of lead: outside workers | ISBN 0-11-883395-2 |

| | | |
|---|---|---|
| EH36 | Work with asbestos cement | ISBN 0-11-885422-4 |
| EH37 | Work with asbestos insulating board | ISBN 0-11-885423-2 |
| EH40 | Occupational exposure limits (updated annually) | ISBN 0-7176-0722-4 |
| EH44 | Dust: general principles of protection | ISBN 0-7176-0507-8 |
| EH47 | Provision, use and maintenance of hygiene facilities for work with asbestos insulation and coatings | ISBN 0-11-885567-0 |
| EH62 | Metalworking fluids – health precautions | ISBN 0-11-885667-7 |
| GS46 | In situ timber treatment using timber preservatives | ISBN 0-11-885413-5 |
| HS(G)37 | Introduction to local exhaust ventilation | ISBN 0-11-882134-2 |
| HS(G)54 | The maintenance examination and testing of local exhaust ventilation | ISBN 0-11-885438-0 |
| HS(G)70 | The control of legionellosis including Legionnaires' Disease | ISBN 0-7176-0451-9 |
| HS(G)77 | COSHH and peripatetic workers | ISBN 0-11-885733-9 |
| HS(G)97 | A step by step guide to COSHH assessment | ISBN 0-11-886379-7 |
| HS(G)108 | CHIP for everyone. Chemicals (Hazard Information and Packaging) Regulations 1993 | ISBN 0-7176-0408-X |
| L5 | Control of Substances Hazardous to Health Regulations 1988 Approved Code of Practice | ISBN 0-7176-0624-4 |
| L8 | The prevention or control of legionellosis (including Legionnaires' Disease) Approved Code of Practice | ISBN 0-7176-0732-1 |
| L9 | The safe use of pesticides for non-agricultural purposes. Approved Code of Practice | ISBN 0-11-885673-1 |
| L11 | A guide to the Asbestos (Licensing) Regulations 1983 | ISBN 0-11-885684-7 |
| L27 | Control of Asbestos at Work Regulations 1987 Approved Code of Practice | ISBN 0-11-882037-0 |
| L37 | Safety data sheets for substances and preparations dangerous for supply. Approved Code of Practice | ISBN 0-7176-0624-4 |
| L38 | Approved guide to the classification and labelling of substances and preparations dangerous for supply | ISBN 0-11-882155-5 |
| | Pesticides: code of practice for the safe use of pesticides on farms and holdings (HSC/MAFF) | ISBN 0-11-242892-4 |
| IND(G)136(L) | COSHH: a brief guide for employers | * |
| IND(G)140(L) | Grain dust in non-agricultural workplaces | * |
| IND(G)151(L) | The complete idiot's guide to CHIP | * |

## *Procedures*
## 15. Safe Systems

| | | |
|---|---|---|
| CS15 | Cleaning and gas freeing of tanks containing flammable residues | ISBN 0-11-883518-1 |
| HS(G)5 | Hot work: welding and cutting on plant containing flammable materials | ISBN 0-11-883299-8 |
| HS(G)85 | Electricity at work: safe working practices | ISBN 0-7176-0442-X |
| IND(G)76 | Safe systems of work | * |
| IND(G)98(L) | Chemical manufacturing: permit to work systems | * |

## 16. Accidents and Emergencies

| | | |
|---|---|---|
| COP42 | Health and Safety (First Aid) Regulations 1981 | ISBN 0-7176-0426-8 |
| FORM F2508 | Report of injury or dangerous occurrence | ISBN 0-7176-0417-9 |
| FORM F2508 | A Report of a case of disease | ISBN 0-7176-0455-1 |
| HSE31 | Everyone's guide to RIDDOR 95 | ISBN 0-7176-1012-8 |
| HS(R)29 | The Dangerous Substances (Notification and Marking of Sites) Regulations 1990 | ISBN 0-11-885435-6 |
| IND(G)4 | First aid at work: general guidance for inclusion in first aid boxes | ISBN 0-11-883958-6 |
| HSE24 | Reporting under RIDDOR | * |
| IND(G)113(L) | Your firm's injury records and how to use them | * |
| IND(G)155(L) | Chemicals – prepared for emergency! | * |

## *People*
## 17. Healthcare

| | | |
|---|---|---|
| HS(G)61 | Surveillance of people exposed to health risks at work | ISBN 0-11-885574-3 |
| HS(G)100 | Prevention of violence to staff in banks and building societies | ISBN 0-7176-0683-X |
| L21 | Management of Health and Safety at Work Regulations Approved Code of Practice 1992 | ISBN 0-7176-0412-8 |
| MS23 | Health aspects of job placement and rehabilitation – advice to employers | ISBN 0-11-885419-4 |
| MS24 | Health surveillance of occupational skin diseases | ISBN 0-11-885583-2 |
| | Health surveillance under COSHH: guidance for employers | ISBN 0-7176-0491-8 |
| | Violence to staff in the health services | ISBN 0-11-883917-9 |
| IND(G)59(L) | Mental health at work | * |
| IND(G)62(L) | Protecting your health at work | * |
| IND(G)63(L) | Passive smoking at work | * |
| IND(G)69(L) | Violence to staff | * |
| IND(G)74(L) | Need advice on occupational health? A practical guide for employers | * |
| IND(G)116(L) | What your doctor needs to know | * |
| IND(G)129(L) | Mental distress at work: first aid measures | * |

## 18. Personal Protective Equipment

| | | |
|---|---|---|
| HS(G)53 | Respiratory protective equipment: a practical guide for users | ISBN 0-11-885522-0 |
| L25 | Personal Protective Equipment at Work Regulations 1992. | ISBN 0-7176-0415-2 |
| | Guidance on Regulations Construction (Head Protection) Regulations 1989 Guidance on Regulations | ISBN 0-11-885503-4 |

## 19. Selection and Training

| | | |
|---|---|---|
| COP26 | Rider operated lift trucks – operator training | ISBN 0-7176-0474-8 |
| GS39 | Training of crane drivers and slingers | ISBN 0-11-883932-2 |
| GS48 | Training and standards of competence for users of chain saws in agriculture, arboriculture and forestry | ISBN 0-11-885575-1 |
| HS(G)83 | Training woodworking machinists | ISBN 0-11-886316-9 |
| L4 | Woodworking Machines Regulations 1974 Guidance on Regulations | ISBN 0-11-885592-1 |
| L21 | Management of Health and Safety at Work Regulations 1992 Approved Code of Practice | ISBN 0-7176-0412-8 |
| IND(G)2(L) | Mind how you go! | * |

## Health and Safety Executive Autofax Index to Selected Publications

Keeping up-to-date with essential health and safety information is now faster and easier than ever before. If you have a phone connected to a fax machine, all you have to do is dial the number shown alongside the publication you require from the list below, or dial 0839 060606 to receive an up-to-date Index page.

Dial 0839 followed by:

| | | Pages |
|---|---|---|
| 060600 | Fortnightly List of HSCHSE Publications | – |
| 060660 | Previous fortnightly list of HSC/HSE publications | – |
| 060601 | 101 Tips to a Safer Business | 9 |
| 060602 | COSHH. A Brief Guide for Employers | 9 |
| 060603 | Drug Abuse at Work: a Guide for Employers | 11 |
| 060604 | Ergonomics at Work | 2 |
| 060605 | First-aid Needs in Your Workplace | 3 |
| 060606 | THIS INDEX PAGE | 2 |
| 060607 | Five Steps to Successful Health and Safety Management | 9 |
| 060608 | Getting to Grips with Manual Handling | 7 |
| 060609 | Health and Safety at Work etc Act. Advice to Employees | 4 |
| 060610 | Health and Safety at Work etc Act. Advice to Employers | 1 |
| 060611 | Health and Safety at Work etc Act. The Act Outlined | 5 |
| 060612 | The Work of the HSE – What HSE can do for you | 12 |
| 060613 | Introducing the Noise at Work Regulations: a Brief Guide to the Requirements of Controlling Noise at Work | 5 |
| 060614 | Legionnaires' Disease | 4 |
| 060615 | Guidance for employers on Musculoskeletal Disorders | 5 |
| 060616 | Guidance for employees on Musculoskeletal Disorders | 5 |
| 060617 | Read the label – How to find out if chemicals are dangerous | 2 |
| 060618 | Managing Asbestos in Workplace Buildings | 6 |
| 060619 | New Health and Safety at Work Regulations | 9 |
| 060620 | Passive Smoking at Work | 7 |
| 060621 | Protecting Your Health at Work | 9 |
| 060622 | Everyone's Guide to RIDDOR 95 | 7 |

# APPENDIX A

# Useful Addresses

## Publications

HSE publications are available from:

HSE Books, PO Box 199, Sudbury, Suffolk CO10 6FS. Tel: 01787 881165, Fax: 01787 313995.

## Information

For general enquiries on workplace health and safety, and to find your way round HSE:

The HSE Infoline. Tel: 0541 545500.

## Other sources of information

British Safety Council, National Safety Centre, 70 Chancellors Road, London W6 9RS. Tel: 0181 741 1231.

Royal Society for the Prevention of Accidents, Cannon House, The Priory, Queensway, Birmingham B4 6BS. Tel: 0121 200 2461.

British Standards Institution, Linford Wood, Milton Keynes MK14 6LE. Tel: 01908 221166.

Trades Union Congress, Congress House, Great Russell Street, London WC1B 3LS. Tel: 0171 636 4030.

Confederation of British Industry, Centre Point, 103 New Oxford Street, London WC1A 1DA. Tel: 0171 370 7400.

# Example of a Health and Safety Policy Statement

## Company Health and Safety Policy Statement

### Stemhouse Maintenance

#### *Objectives*

Stemhouse Maintenance is a small contractor's business in the construction industry. We concentrate on jobbing and maintenance work. We are four partners, and subcontract work to self-employed operators when the need arises. All machinery is hired. We have an office at base, but no working premises of our own. All our work is done on other people's sites.

This system of work raises four major concerns for us. First is the problem of fully grasping the risks and safe procedures of the sites we are going to work on. Secondly, we have the duty to look after the safety of a workteam which sometimes includes operatives freshly recruited for the job. Thirdly, we frequently work on sites in which other employees and the public at large are in close proximity. Fourthly, we use hired machinery which is operated by contracted labour some of whom we may have engaged for the first time.

To organise a system of work in these conditions which is safe, protects the health of all involved, and takes due care for the protection of anyone else likely to be affected, requires two things. We, the partners, must set the example. If we want the people we bring onto the job to work safely we, the partners, must know what the risks are, and what are the safe procedures. We must then make sure they are all properly briefed and equipped to follow them.

We are all aware that, to keep abreast of these demands, experience of construction work is not enough on its own. We need to know the Construction (Design and Management) Regulations, and the other detailed construction Regulations. The legal controls over waste disposal and environmental protection must also be covered, as well as the basic legislation setting out general management standards in health and safety. All the partners, including the one acting as safety assistant, who already holds an IOSH Diploma, have studied these.

#### *Organisation*

In our company the four partners share the responsibilities for managing health, safety and environmental protection. Mary Mills, one of the partners, reports all accidents under the RIDDOR Regulations. She prepares the safety policy statement, the COSHH, the general workplace assessment of risks, and other statutory risk assessments. She arranges the documentation for agreeing safe working procedures with the client or contractor for whom we are engaged.

She also takes charge of providing the method statement for every site we work on getting it mutually endorsed with the client or main contractor and ensuring that the site manager and all people working on it are fully briefed on their responsibilities under it.

On each working site one of the partners takes responsibility for the safe organisation, operator briefing, condition of tools, handling of personal protective equipment, provision of warning signs, administering first-aid, fire and other emergency procedures, keeping records of first-aid treatment and accidents, and general safety management. This includes watching for evidence of injury and health hazard, and checking that waste is properly consigned and despatched.

Everyone working on our contracts receives and is briefed on a code of safe practice, a section of which explains his personal responsibility to act on the advice in the code, and to report any evidence of hazards or unsafe practice without delay.

Thomas Mills takes charge of formal training for newcomers to our company, and for briefing sessions on new programmes of work. He also has the responsibility of checking the competence of operatives handling powered tools or vehicles. He also reports monthly to the other partners. James McCuster undertakes a monthly audit of all equipment, warning notices and official records, and reports directly to the partner.

## Arrangements

### Instruction, rules, procedures, warning notices etc.

#### Management

Mary Mills prepares the policy statement in conjunction with the other partner. We review it at six-monthly intervals, and additionally whenever necessary if important changes are made. We monitor general standards on a rotating list, ensuring all areas are covered in time for the policy statement review. Comments from operatives are encouraged. Similar arrangements are made for COSHH and the other statutory risk assessments. The latest versions of these are attached to this policy statement as Appendices A and C. She also prepares our method statements.

#### Method statements

Every person working with us on a contract must be fully briefed on the methods and procedures set out in the method statement, and the safety precautions required, including the working relations with the client, planning supervisor, principal contractor or other contractor.

#### Safety notices and signs

Site managers are responsible for delivering, setting up, and collecting notices and signs, and ensuring they are appropriate to the needs.

*Monitoring*

One of the partners is responsible for regularly checking all our PPE, signs and notices, delivery vehicles, fire-fighting and first-aid equipment. He reports monthly to the other partners on the state of the maintenance. Mrs Mills gives a similar report on the written records.

*Personal Protective Equipment*

We provide appropriate protective clothing, helmet, gloves, footwear, respirators, hearing protection and safety glasses as necessary. On receipt, operatives are instructed in their duty to use the equipment when required to, and to report and hand in immediately defective equipment. Similar instructions are recorded on their pocket codes.

*Reporting and recording accidents etc.*

Operatives are instructed directly and in the pocket code to report every near-miss, accident, including first-aid treatment, and evidence of possible health problems, to the site manager without delay, and to ensure that it is recorded. The site manager has the duty to inform Mary Mills, in turn. Any potential defect in equipment, work processes or other hazard on the worksite, must also be reported to the site manager for onward reference to Mary Mills.

*Emergency action – first aid*

A first-aid kit is taken to every site unless it is explicitly provided by a main contractor. Site managers are responsible for handling all injuries, major and minor, and ensuring procedures are followed.

*Emergency action – fire risks*

Whenever a job involves a fire hazard, for example using flammable materials, operatives are instructed not to start work if fire-fighting equipment is not available. Site managers must also brief operatives before the job begins about the drill for fire prevention and escape. One section of the pocket code sets out these responsibilities.

*Health hazards*

The attention of everyone working for us is directed to the sections of the pocket code about health hazards. Site managers question operatives on possible health complaints, as appropriate. Anyone finding evidence of skin, chest, ear or other health trouble is instructed to report the matter without delay to the site manager. The COSHH assessment sheets for health hazards likely to be met on our work are available for inspection by staff, and are attached to this policy statement as Appendix C.

*Environmental hazards*

Site managers regularly check that no environmental hazard is created. Wastes must be managed according to the Approved Code of Practice. Everyone on the site must be alert to ensure no statutory nuisances occur. Operatives' attention is directed to the section on the environment in the pocket code.

## Information and consultation

*Operatives' information*

Every operative is issued with our pocket safety code and the appropriate sections of it are referred to in the briefing before the start of any new work process. It is a condition of the contract that the code is carried by the operative at all times whilst working, since sections of it give advice on action in emergency. One section of the code emphasises the need for special care and attention for residents in dwellings in which we are engaged in contract work, and to report promptly any inconvenience.

*Consultation*

Any suggestions for amending or adding to the company's policy statement or pocket code of safe working, as noted in the code, are welcomed. A copy of the pocket code is attached as Appendix B.

## Training and briefing

*Training*

On each new job operatives are briefed on the hazards likely to be met, and the methods of dealing with any problems arising. They are referred as appropriate to the relevant sections in their pocket codes. Operatives working for us for the first time are separately briefed about their role in the company's broad policy for safety. Operatives using mechanical tools must have given documentary evidence of their competence to handle them, before being allowed to work them.

## *Appendices to the policy statement*

A: general assessment of risks

B: Company pocket code of safe working

C: Other statutory assessments, COSHH, etc.

Signed:

*Mary Mills, MIOSH*

*David Walkman M.I.S.M.*

*George Mills*

*J. Mc Custer MIIRSH*

Managing Partners

*17ᵗʰ March 1995.*

# Concluding comments

## Making the points hit home

### 1. Presentation

As a heading it is sufficient to give the company's name and address, and the title 'Health and Safety Policy Statement'. The impression it makes will be enhanced if it is smartly and professionally presented.

More important still, are the contents of the opening section on policy, or policy objectives as the Robens Committee described it. If this brings the company to life and clearly involves both managers and operatives, it will attract attention when it is posted up. The remainder of the statement need not be put up on show, a reference to where it can be obtained at the end of the opening statement will be sufficient.

The statement, including the section posted up, needs to be signed and dated. The signature should be that of the chief executive on behalf of the employer. In a partnership each of the partners should sign. The date is important. An undated report, as much as one dated many years previously, raises the suspicion that the policy has been marooned in a cupboard for some years.

### 2. Making the statement thorough but brief

Customers, clients and principal contractors, no less than safety representatives or inspectors, when asking to see a policy statement, want something that gets down to brass tacks quickly. They want enough evidence to see that the key points of safety management and control are covered and that they relate to a real situation, not a handout.

This can be done by giving actual examples of key controls and management procedures whose authenticity can be quickly checked by an examination of the workplace. Once the veracity of these has been established, many of the details can be assumed.

Much of the relevant information on individual risks and protective measures can be stored in the general workplace assessment of risks, which has also to be in written form in companies with five or more employees. This can be added to the policy statement as an appendix. The key information becomes available without cluttering up the main policy statement with details.

### 3. Bringing the Report to life

The Robens Committee proposed that the opening section of the policy statement should be described as 'policy objectives'. They wanted to make the point that policy was dynamic, not static. Its purpose was not just to set targets, but to help rally the support needed to reach them. One important objective was to make the managers and employees conscious of their join responsibility to take health and safety seriously.

There are no hard and fast rules as to how this can be done. One suggestion is to convey briefly an overview of the company – its characteristic risks and its plans for mobilising support for its strategy to overcome them. This can be followed, for example, by a reference to a prize won by the company during the year for its health and safety record, or a special course run for its supervisors and safety representatives to up-date them on health protection. As people start reading the statement on the notice-board it will become clear to them that it refers to a real place with real problems and real people, not a list of abstracts from a law-book.

## 4. Make sure the evidence in the report is checkable

Drafters of the policy statement should ensure that any assertion about people, procedures, publications, equipment or processes made in it can be demonstrated as factual. Evidence on the shop-floor, in the records, in training briefs or from the people involved, must be readily available for checking, should anyone raise the question.

## 5. Ensure protection of environmental risks is included

The 1974 Health & Safety at Work Act does not refer to inclusion of the protection of the environment or non-employees in the written policy statement. In practice businesses large and small have responsibilities for both. The prevention of nuisance to neighbours from, for example, noise or waste disposal can be a problem for many small firms. So, too, is the protection of the public and other employees in construction work on roads or buildings. It is sensible for these issues to be covered in the policy statement. The employer has a legal duty to keep them under control.

## 6. Pocket briefs

For employees who have to work in small numbers on detached sites, a useful means of providing them with on-the-spot guidance is the pocket brief. In isolated situations, advice on where to ring for help in emergency and reminders about basic protection for eyes, hearing, skin contamination and concern for the public can often meet an immediate need. The pocket brief, added as an Appendix to the policy statement, can be useful evidence that practical information on safe working is being provided for such workers.

# APPENDIX C

# COSHH
# Assessment Record

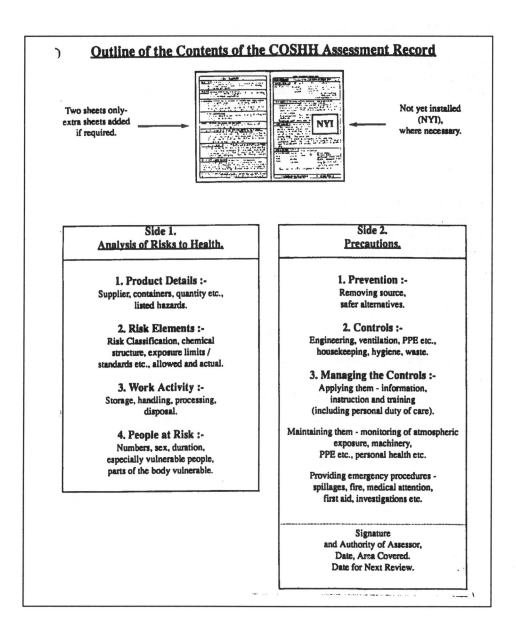

## Outline of the Contents of the COSHH Assessment Record

Two sheets only-
extra sheets added
if required.

NYI

Not yet installed
(NYI),
where necessary.

### Side 1.
### Analysis of Risks to Health.

**1. Product Details :-**
Supplier, containers, quantity etc.,
listed hazards.

**2. Risk Elements :-**
Risk Classification, chemical
structure, exposure limits /
standards etc., allowed and actual.

**3. Work Activity :-**
Storage, handling, processing,
disposal.

**4. People at Risk :-**
Numbers, sex, duration,
especially vulnerable people,
parts of the body vulnerable.

### Side 2.
### Precautions.

**1. Prevention :-**
Removing source,
safer alternatives.

**2. Controls :-**
Engineering, ventilation, PPE etc.,
housekeeping, hygiene, waste.

**3. Managing the Controls :-**
Applying them - information,
instruction and training
(including personal duty of care).

Maintaining them - monitoring of atmospheric
exposure, machinery,
PPE etc., personal health etc.

Providing emergency procedures -
spillages, fire, medical attention,
first aid, investigations etc.

Signature
and Authority of Assessor,
Date, Area Covered.
Date for Next Review.

## COSHH Assessment Record Form

### Side 1 - Analysis of Risks to Health

| COSHH Assessment Reference: | CW/12/96 |
|---|---|

| Product Details |
|---|
| Substance Name/ Name of Supplier: Quantity/Containers: Suppliers Data Sheet/Listed Hazards |
| **Domestos / Lever Industrial Ltd: 1 gall professional pack/ polythene bottles:** **Product Handling Sheet 93/4300/R55189 /** **Sodium Hypochlorite (corrosive)** **Sodium Hydroxide (very corrosive)** |

| Risk Elements and Exposure |
|---|
| Risk Classification: Areas of body vulnerable: Exposure limit/standard - Prescribed, Actual |
| **Irritant (contains caustic soda): must not be used with any other product - this could produce chlorine.** **Eyes and skin vulnerable. Could also be harmful if ingested.** **No recommendation for monitoring exposure given on Product Handling Sheet.** |

| Work Activity |
|---|
| Storage: Handling: Processing: Disposal |
| **Four bottles stored in locked broom cupboard.** **All 12 lavatories in Crossways Residential Home are cleaned** **Cleaning staff dispense Domestos with measure nightly.** |

| People at Risk (Directly or Indirectly) |
|---|
| Parts of body exposed: Duration: Sex: Age: Specially vulnerable |
| **Direct: Potentially skin and eyes of two cleaning staff, female, aged 21 and 32 - not specially vulnerable.** **Indirect: Residents. Undiluted Domestos must not be left where residents could come into contact with it. Because of the dilution of the measured quantity for cleaning, residents are not judged to be at risk when using the lavatory.** |

| Add extra sheets if necessary | Precautions overleaf |
|---|---|

**Side 2 - Precautions**

| Prevention |
|---|
| Elimination or substitution:<br>**Other cleaning agents are less efficient and are also potentially hazardous.** |

| Controls |
|---|
| Engineering: (automation, ventilation, LEV etc.)<br>**Lavatory windows are ledt open for ventilation. no other cleaning product is used in conjunction. Only cleaning staff hold key to broom cupboard.** |
| Personal Protection: (skin creams, clothing, respirators etc. Equipment repair/storage/cleaning).<br>**Rubber gloves. Spare pack kept in kitchen.** |
| Hygiene: (toilets, food/smoking controls)<br>**Employees eat and smoke only in the messroom.** |
| Disposal: (clean product, clear workspace, safe waste disposal)<br>**Empty bottles are washed out with water before disposal.** |

| Managing the Controls |
|---|
| (warning signs, work rules, training, PPE use, handling, personal hygiene, health surveillance, dealing with emergencies, employee duty of care)<br>**The use of hazardous substances is covered in standard training provided for all employees. The proprietor of the home, a qualified nursing sister, provides close supervision. Staff are instructed to keep the cupboard containing the Domestos locked, and to ensure that the bottles are locked away immediately after use.** |

| Monitoring the Controls |
|---|
| (audits, examinations, testing of equipment, risk exposures, ill health, control deficiencies)<br>**Surveillance by the proprietor gives adequate cover.** |

| Dealing with Control Failure |
|---|
| (spillages, fire, first-aid, medical care)<br>**Cleaners have been instructed in first-aid and the action to be taken in case of spillage. (Carefully mop up wearing apron - use warning signs and barrier to exclude residents.)** |

Signature and Authority of Assessor:      Date:      Area Covered:

D.W. Simkiss RGN MISM        4 Dec 96   Crossways Residential
   Proprietor .                         Home

Date for next Review: **4 Dec 98**

# SAFETY DATA SHEET

## 1. IDENTIFICATION OF THE SUBSTANCE/PREPARATION AND COMPANY

| | PRODUCT NAME: | EMERGENCY TELEPHONE NO: |
|---|---|---|
| LEVER INDUSTRIAL LIMITED<br>PO BOX 100<br>RUNCORN<br>CHESHIRE<br>WA7 3JZ<br>TEL 0928 719000 | **DOMESTOS** | 0928 701000<br><br>REF NO: 93/4300/R55189<br><br>ISSUE DATE. 17/06/94 |

| PHYSICAL FORM:<br>Viscous liquid | PRODUCT TYPE:<br>Hypochlorite bleach | CONTAINER:<br>Plastic Can |
|---|---|---|

## 2. COMPOSITION/INFORMATION ON INGREDIENTS

| | | | OEL | |
|---|---|---|---|---|
| NAME | | RANGE | STEL | TWA |
| WATER | > 75% | | | |
| SODIUM HYPOCHLORITE | 1-5% | Corrosive | | |
| SODIUM CHLORIDE | 1-5% | | | |
| AMINE OXIDE | 1-5% | Irritant | | |
| SODIUM HYDROXIDE | < 1% | Very corrosive | 2 | |

STEL - Short Term Exposure Level. TWA - 8hrs Time Weighted Average.
OELs are UK standard, expressed as mg/m³. They are Occupational Exposure Standards, unless marked *, which indicate Maximum Exposure Level.

## 3. HAZARD IDENTIFICATION  Irritant to skin and eyes.

## 4. FIRST AID MEASURES

| EYE: | Wash immediately with copious amounts of water and obtain medical attention. |
|---|---|
| SKIN: | Wash skin thoroughly with water. |
| INGESTION: | Remove material from mouth. Drink 1 or 2 glasses of water (or milk) and obtain medical attention. |
| INHALATION: | REMOVE FROM SOURCE OF EXPOSURE AND OBTAIN MEDICAL ATTENTION WITHOUT DELAY. |
| EQUIPMENT AT WORK PLACE: | Eye and skin washing facilities. Drench shower if handling large amounts. |

## 5. FIRE FIGHTING MEASURES

FLAMMABILITY:   Not flammable

| SUITABLE EXTINGUISHERS·<br>Any can be used. | EXPLOSIVE HAZARDS:<br>None known. |
|---|---|
| EXTINGUISHERS NOT TO BE USED:<br>None. | |
| SPECIAL PROTECTIVE EQUIPMENT:<br>Breathing apparatus should be worn when tackling fires involving this product. | HAZARDOUS COMBUSTION PRODUCTS:<br>Toxic and irritant fumes may be given off when heated to decomposition. |

Page 1 of 2

Continued ☞

☞ Continued

| PRODUCT NAME: DOMESTOS | | REF NO: 93/4303/R55189 |
|---|---|---|

**6. ACCIDENTAL RELEASE MEASURES**

| PERSONAL PROTECTION | As for Exposure Controls. |
|---|---|
| SPILLAGE CLEAN-UP | Absorb large spillages into an inert material (eg sand) and collect together in suitably labelled containers for disposal at an approved site (1980 Special Waste Regs). Wash residues away to drain with water. |

**7. HANDLING AND STORAGE**

| HANDLING | Do not mix with acidic materials, as this will cause the rapid evolution of chlorine gas. |
|---|---|
| STORAGE | Store in the original sealed containers under dry conditions, away from acidic materials. Avoid extremes of temperature. Do not overtighten cap. |

**8. EXPOSURE CONTROLS**
Protective goggles should be worn.

**9. PHYSICAL AND CHEMICAL PROPERTIES**

APPEARANCE: Liquid

| SOLUBILITY IN WATER: Miscible | BOILING POINT °C: Not applicable |
|---|---|
| pH: 13 | FLASH POINT °C: Not applicable |
| VISCOSITY AT 20°C: 150 cPa/s | DENSITY: 1.078 g/cc |

**10. STABILITY AND REACTIVITY**   Contact with acids will cause the rapid release of chlorine gas.

**11. TOXICOLOGICAL INFORMATION**

| EYE: | Causes irritation. |
|---|---|
| SKIN: | Can cause irritation. |
| INGESTION: | Causes irritation. |
| INHALATION: | Causes irritation, and may cause bronchospasm in chlorine sensitive individuals. |

**12. ECOLOGICAL INFORMATION**   The only potential hazard is from the alkalinity of the product. To safeguard the environment the bleach breaks down to common salt, oxygen and other harmless substances.

**13. DISPOSAL CONSIDERATIONS**

| CONTENTS: | Observe current rules of the local authority. |
|---|---|
| EMPTY CONTAINERS: | Observe current rules of the local authority. |

**14. TRANSPORT INFORMATION**

UN NO AND PACKAGING GROUP:   Non dangerous material.

**15. REGULATORY INFORMATION**

| R36/38 | Irritating to eyes and skin. |
|---|---|
| S2 | Keep out of reach of children. |
| S26 | In case of contact with eyes, rinse immediately with plenty of water and seek medical advice. |

**16. OTHER INFORMATION**
Warning. Do not use together with other products. May release dangerous gases (chlorine). Handle and apply only as recommended.

# COSHH Assessment Check List
## for Identifying Risks and Checking Precautions Taken.
# 1. Hazardous Substance(s) :-

| (Areas and Items to be Inspected) | (Space for Notes and Comments) |
|---|---|
| **Official Risks and Prescribed Controls :-** | |
| Name of product, supplier, quantity, containers, listed hazards :- | |
| Chemical structure, risk classification :- | |
| Exposure limits/standards - allowed, actual :- | |
| **Treatment in the Workplace :-** | |
| Storage :- | |
| Handling :- | |
| Processing :- | |
| Disposal :- | |
| **People at Risk :-** | |
| Numbers, duration, sex :- | |
| Parts of the body vulnerable :- | |
| Especially vulnerable people :- | |
| **Other Hazards Involved :-** | |
| **Other Concerns :-** | |

12

## 2. Risks - the Precautions Taken :-

### Prevention of Risk (First Option) :-

Substitution
Change of process

### Engineering Controls Over Risk Areas (Second Option) :-

Automation
Screening
Ventilation

### Use of PPE (Third Option) :-

Correct type
Fits well
Used safely
Storage
Cleaning
Repair
Reporting defects

### Hygiene :-

Clean workplaces
Washing and toilet
Eating and smoking
only in allocated rooms
Separate accommodation
for PPE and personal clothing

### Controls Over Disposal :-

Clean Product
Clear workplace
Safe waste disposal

### Incidental Non-Health Risks :-

### Checking People at Risk :-

Identified
Protected
Recorded

### Instruction, Information and Training

Controls and action
Use of equipment
Personal hygiene
Reporting hazards
Warning signs
Training and briefing -
organised, documented, records kept

## 3. Monitoring the Risks and Controls :-

New equipment, substances
   - exposure measurement
Inspections and testing
   - airborne exposures
   - mechanical equipment
   - PPE
   - workplace hygiene
   - workers health
   - recorded

## 4. Emergency Procedures :-

Contamination
Ill-health
Other emergencies
Equipment, records
Training

## 5. Other, Non-Tabulated, Problems :-

| Name | Department | Hazard | Date |
|------|------------|--------|------|
|      |            |        |      |

# APPENDIX D

# Definitions of Major Injuries, Dangerous Occurrences and Diseases

## Reportable major injuries are:

- fracture other than to fingers, thumbs or toes;
- amputation; dislocation of the shoulder, hip, knee or spine;
- loss of sight (temporary or permanent);
- chemical or hot metal burn to the eye or any penetrating injury to the eye;
- injury resulting from an electric shock or electrical burn leading to unconsciousness or requiring resuscitation or admittance to hospital for more than 24 hours;
- any other injury: leading to hypothermia, heat-induced illness or unconsciousness; or requiring resuscitation; or requiring admittance to hospital for more than 24 hours;
- unconsciousness caused by asphyxia or exposure to harmful substance or biological agent;
- acute illness requiring medical treatment, or loss of consciousness arising from absorption of any substance by inhalation, ingestion or through the skin;
- acute illness requiring medical treatment where there is reason to believe that this resulted from exposure to a biological agent or its toxins or infected material.

## Reportable dangerous occurrences are:

- collapse, overturning or failure of load-bearing parts of lifts and lifting equipment;
- explosion, collapse or bursting of any closed vessel or associated pipework;
- failure of any freight container in any of its load-bearing parts;
- plant or equipment coming into contact with overhead power lines;
- electrical short circuit or overload causing fire or explosion;
- any unintentional explosion, misfire, failure of demolition to cause the intended collapse, projection of material beyond a site boundary, injury caused by an explosion;
- accidental release of a biological agent likely to cause severe human illness;
- failure of industrial radiography or irradiation equipment to de-energize or return to its safe position after the intended exposure period;
- malfunction of breathing apparatus while in use or during testing immediately before use;
- failure or endangering of diving equipment, the trapping of a diver, an explosion near a diver, or an uncontrolled ascent;

- collapse or partial collapse of a scaffold over 5 metres high, or erected near water where there could be a risk of drowning after a fall;
- unintended collision of a train with any vehicle;
- dangerous occurrence at a well (other than a water well); dangerous occurrence at a pipeline;
- failure of any load-bearing fairground equipment, or derailment or unintended collision of cars or trains;
- a road tanker carrying a dangerous substance overturns, suffers serious damage, catches fire or the substance is released;
- a dangerous substance being conveyed by road is involved in a fire or released;

*The following dangerous occurrences are reportable except in relation to offshore workplaces:*

- unintended collapse of: any building or structure under construction, alteration or demolition where over five tonnes of material falls; a wall or floor in a place of work; any falsework;
- explosion or fire causing suspension of normal work for over 24 hours;
- sudden, uncontrolled release in a building of: 100 kg or more of flammable liquid; 10 kg of flammable liquid above its boiling point; 10 kg or more of flammable gas; or of 500 kg of these substances if the release is in the open air;
- accidental release of any substance which may damage health.

*Note: additional categories of dangerous occurrences apply to mines, quarries, relevant transport systems (railways etc.) and offshore workplaces.*

## Reportable diseases include:

- certain poisonings;
- some skin diseases such as occupational dermatitis, skin cancer, chrome ulcer, oil folliculitis/acne;
- lung diseases including: occupational asthma, farmer's lung, pneumoconiosis, asbestosis, mesothelioma;
- infections such as: leptospirosis; hepatitis; tuberculosis; anthrax; legionellosis and tetanus;
- other conditions such as: occupational cancer; certain musculoskeletal disorders; decompression illness and hand-arm vibration syndrome.

The full list of reportable diseases can be found in the detailed guide to the Regulations and in the pad of report forms, or simply ring HSE to check. They are related to particular work activities.

# Index